This book i
- ❖ Fee
    rela
- ❖ Worry that you are **not attractive enough**
- ❖ **Don't always feel loved**
- ❖ Feel that **sex has become a predictable routine** and lost that special spark
- ❖ Dream of having a **heart-to-heart connection** with your man
- ❖ Yearn to express your deepest feelings and to **be understood**
- ❖ **Feel frustrated** and **dissatisfied** deep down
- ❖ **Are excited about becoming a magical, sexy woman** for your man

By the end of this book, you will:
- ❖ Have the tools to **transform your relationship** so that you **feel supported and understood**
- ❖ Be **excited about your relationship** and look forward to a **joyful and fulfilling love adventure together**
- ❖ Blossom into a **confident, radiant woman** and feel attractive and **comfortable in your own skin**

- ❖ Learn how to **relax and melt during lovemaking,** knowing that you are an amazing lover
- ❖ Look forward to spending a **whole weekend** making **passionate love** with your man
- ❖ Learn ways to create **deep intimacy** and **rekindle passion with your man**
- ❖ Learn how to inspire your man to **cherish, support,** and **adore** you
- ❖ Appreciate the **erotic beauty** of your body
- ❖ Feel free and **confident to express all of your feelings** with your man and to be loved for the woman you are

How to make HIM *fall in* LOVE *with* YOU *all over again*

7 WEEKS TO MORE INTIMACY AND DELICIOUS SEX IN YOUR RELATIONSHIP

TARISHA TOUROK

BALBOA
PRESS
A DIVISION OF HAY HOUSE

Copyright © 2013 Tarisha Tourok

All rights reserved. No part of this book may be used or reproduced by any means, graphic, electronic, or mechanical, including photocopying, recording, taping or by any information storage retrieval system without the written permission of the publisher except in the case of brief quotations embodied in critical articles and reviews.

Balboa Press books may be ordered through booksellers or by contacting:

Balboa Press
A Division of Hay House
1663 Liberty Drive
Bloomington, IN 47403
www.balboapress.com.au
1-(877) 407-4847

ISBN: 978-1-4525-0935-8 (sc)
ISBN: 978-1-4525-0938-9 (e)

Because of the dynamic nature of the Internet, any web addresses or links contained in this book may have changed since publication and may no longer be valid. The views expressed in this work are solely those of the author and do not necessarily reflect the views of the publisher, and the publisher hereby disclaims any responsibility for them.

The author of this book does not dispense medical advice or prescribe the use of any technique as a form of treatment for physical, emotional, or medical problems without the advice of a physician, either directly or indirectly. The intent of the author is only to offer information of a general nature to help you in your quest for emotional and spiritual well-being. In the event you use any of the information in this book for yourself, which is your constitutional right, the author and the publisher assume no responsibility for your actions.

Any people depicted in stock imagery provided by Thinkstock are models, and such images are being used for illustrative purposes only.
Certain stock imagery © Thinkstock.

Printed in the United States of America

Balboa Press rev. date: 03/19/2013

WARNING: *This is not just another book on relationships* giving you advice on what to say to your man or how to look at him in a way you hope will make him love you more. This book focuses on who you are in the relationship rather than on what you do. We can change our behaviour, but if we don't change what we believe about ourselves and life, nothing will really change.

Simply adjusting our behaviour can be superficial, manipulative, and hard to sustain. Some books on relationships tell you, for example, not to criticise your man and to appreciate him. How on earth are we supposed to do that if we feel that he doesn't care, and he behaves in ways that hurt us? We need to first understand why our partner is doing what he is doing and find a way to step into a state of love and appreciation. Only then can we authentically appreciate him.

This applies to all areas of our lives. That's why people struggle with losing weight. They go on a diet, and it works for a while. Then they gain all their weight back and more. It's because their inner belief structure and motivation hasn't changed, and without it, sustaining the diet is very hard if not impossible.

I don't ask you to will yourself into behaving differently. I offer you the blueprint for changing the way you are with your man so that you naturally start to relate to him in a different way. This is the foundation on which it will be easy for you to create a harmonious relationship. I will also reveal secrets about men and the art of building a loving, intimate relationship, but the foundation is the most important part.

You can apply the teachings from this book to any of your relationships, not just your intimate relationship. The foundational principles of this book will support you in changing your relationships with your colleagues, your children, your relatives, and, most importantly, yourself. It will empower you to live the life of your dreams by creating the world and life you want.

This book is not a quick fix; you will need to do the work and uncover what blocks you from having the relationship you always wanted. All the answers are inside you.

I will share with you how to reclaim your power and create the relationship of your dreams, without trying to force your man to change.

Two persons, neither independent nor dependent but in a tremendous synchronicity, as if breathing for each other, one soul in two bodies—whenever that happens, love has happened.
Osho

To my beloved mystic, Osho, for my life.

To my beautiful, dazzling daughter, Nika Lucia, for teaching me love and patience.

To Beath Davis for inspiring me and showing me the truth of who I am.

To Kamal Starr for loving me, supporting me, and sharing the journey with me.

To Bogdan Derevyanko for his wisdom, friendship, and invaluable contribution.

Contents

1. Overture xiii
2. Yes, Beautiful, the Power Is in Your Hands! 1
3. The Most Powerful Way to Turn Your
   Relationship Around—Ready? Jump! 21
4. Let's Fill Up Your Love Tanks! 37
5. Make Him Your Hero 59
6. Become a Magnetic Sensual Goddess 75
7. The Way to Delicious Sex 93
8. Ancient, Yet Simple, Tools to Have All the
   Pleasure You Desire 123
9. Finale 139

OVERTURE

The art of love is an emotional midwifery. WE hold each other as we emerge together into the light of a new life, both exhilarating and terrifying.
Marianne Williamson

I love *love*. I admire *men*. I am a *woman*.

Love is so precious. Oh, the feeling of being completely in love. That sparkle in the eyes, the way that everything makes sense, the fact that there is purpose to everything... The sun shines so much brighter, and even the rain is romantic.

The power of love!

It transforms the world, the whole experience of my life. The delicious tingling in my body, the expectation of seeing him, and the delight of looking into his eyes. The connection beyond all words is seeing into each other beyond our physical forms. Oh, and not to forget the joy of touching and smelling him long after he's gone. I'm expanded. Somehow my body is three times its size, vibrantly alive, and pulsing with love, every cell throbbing with life. And there is this absolute certainty that life is beautiful. Love is an animating force that gives meaning and coherence to everything.

My fascination with men started with my dad. He was so strong and reliable, and when mum would give up on my crying, he could easily calm me down. And his voice: Deep. Powerful. Magnetic. So manly.

I admire the ability of men to put their values above their emotions; the support and trust I feel when I am around them; and their qualities of strength, focused purpose, and honour.

Yes, I'm a complicated woman with all my moods jumping up and down, going from ecstatic bliss to dark and tragic. And I love it.

Up to five years of age I thought I was a boy. My parents so wanted to have a boy that I naturally assumed I was one. I thought of the female race as stupid and weak, untrustworthy, and constant complainers—nothing to be proud of. When my brother was born and I realised the difference, I was devastated. Who am I now? Do I have to belong to this weak, unreliable sex? It was a painful wake-up call, but I decided not to take on qualities I found repulsive and focused on being the best boy of all the girls.

I succeeded. I ran faster than all the boys, did all the scary stuff like testing explosives in the house, and became friends only with boys. Girls didn't deserve my attention. In my first twenty-six years of my life, I think I was the best boy of all the girls. Well done, Tarisha!

But then came a point in my life when something inside started to ache. I was disconnected from myself. I didn't like myself. It was painful to be in a relationship but not feel connected and understood on a deep intimate level by my partner. Two years into my first marriage I started to wonder—where did the passion go? Where was my perfect lover whom I dreamt of when I was seventeen—the one who would take me on an ecstatic love adventure? I was achieving great results in my career, yet I felt that routine took away my joy and passion. I was miserable. I didn't feel loved, and I felt stuck in my relationship. It was terrifying to feel so completely alone while being with a man I loved.

What now? Where was I to go? What was I to do? I had a yearning to create a deep intimate relationship full of love and growth, but I didn't know how.

Maybe it was the time for flight? Off I went, to India. That's how I started my discovery of myself. Am I really a woman? Is it really good to be a woman? Are women not really a weaker, less intelligent race? Should I be proud to be a woman? Really? My whole world was turned upside down. Seeing a woman as a goddess? Honouring the goddess in me? Recognising a woman as a creative force in the universe? And what was I to do with the idea that men are made stronger physically in order to protect precious women, the force of love and life on this earth? You must be kidding. It took me a while to get my head around all these concepts and really feel them in my body. Oh boy!

I'm a *Woman*! Mum, I'm so proud I was born a woman, thank you. I'm sorry I disappointed you, but I'm so grateful for the disappointment I caused. Wow, and apparently, my body is beautiful. These strange people in India even insisted that I'm beautiful! My god, life is a miracle! I love myself, I love myself, I love myself. After all, I'm not a mistake. I'm a goddess! And I choose to be a goddess of love and joy.

Now my question is, "What can be created between a god and a goddess?" That's what I want to explore.

I'm blessed with the relationship I have, now. And it took a lot of work to come to this place.

With my partner, now, I feel loved, cherished, and understood. He makes an effort to make me happy, and he considers my desires and needs. It gives me a feeling that I am the *one*. I love to see the spark of desire in his eyes and his lust for my body.

I now understand that I *had* to go through the pain of divorce and get over the denial of my own femininity to become a radiant woman and discover my magnetic sensual power. How else would I experience the magic of complete openness and sexual ecstasy with my beloved? The intensity of almost palpable passion and connection I now experience is indescribable. It is such a pleasure to feel erotically beautiful and enjoy deep intimacy in my life.

I feel deeply penetrated by love, and my heart melts. We grow together. We explore uncharted territories and become more and more complete in our own beings.

The authenticity of our communication is remarkable. I never dreamt of sharing exactly what I feel and want and being given the space to be my true self. My man is present with me and this makes me feel safe to open up. Of course we have arguments and some explosive emotions, but this helps our relationship grow. What's amazing is that I don't think of being somewhere else—it feels so deep and meaningful to be right here.

I've written this book because I don't want you to go through the pain of failed relationships, an empty heart, and having children without a father. Our children need to see love to learn how to love. If parents do not love each other, it'll be harder for children to have loving relationships in their lives. They need role models. If we are not happy in our relationship, that's what our children learn—that family and partnership is not a happy place to be.

I've written this book as an expression of my intention to live my life in full bloom and support people to live their lives in full bloom.

I've written this book to:

- ❖ Help you keep your family together where children flourish in the atmosphere of love, trust, and respect.
- ❖ Give you the tools to transform your relationship so that you become excited about your relationship and look forward to a joyful and fulfilling love adventure together.
- ❖ Help you to blossom into a confident, radiant woman who feels attractive and comfortable in her own skin.
- ❖ Teach you how to relax and melt during lovemaking, knowing that you are an amazing lover.
- ❖ Teach you ways to create deep intimacy and reignite passion with your man.
- ❖ Show you how to inspire your man to cherish, support, and adore you.
- ❖ Encourage you to step into your full power and love yourself just the way you are.

I recognise that sometimes the best thing might be to physically separate from our partner and open up to new possibilities for love. However, we need to do this from an empowered state, with a sense of deep care for our partner and our children. First, we need to find out what's not working and what we can do to change the unhappy dynamics in our relationship. Only after we have given 100 percent of our effort and commitment and have realised that we can't possibly fulfil each other's needs should we start considering other options. We make decisions rooted in our and our partner's sense of inherent goodness and value. We honour the divine expression in our partner and act for the highest good of all involved, without blaming and engaging into unnecessary damaging drama.

Let's begin the journey.

How to Read This Book

This book is structured for you to read one chapter a week. A week will give you enough time to assimilate the material and do the weekly practices and homeplays.

You can just read the book without doing any exercises, but that will only leave you with practical knowledge. To transform your relationship, you need to embrace and embody your knowledge, and that's why I strongly recommend committing to doing all the practices. Your experience may surprise you and reveal something totally unexpected.

Prepare a special journal to work through this book as I'll take you through a number of reflection exercises.

I mention some of my clients in this book. I changed their names and some circumstances to preserve their confidentiality. I'm grateful to my clients for teaching me and trusting me, for committing to themselves to uncover their true nature, and for relentlessly working towards love and harmony in their lives.

WEEK 1

Yes, Beautiful, the Power Is in Your Hands!

> *Every woman is a face of the Goddess.*
> Janet and Stewart Farrar

Remember the Love and Passion You Had in the Beginning

Perhaps in your mind you can remember that unique feeling of being in love with your man, but in your heart the spark now somehow seems lost. Yet something deep down tells you the fire is not completely out; there are embers that can be fanned into flames.

It's time to take a brief journey into the past. Imagine being there with your man right now. When we re-create the past in our imagination and use present tense when talking about the events that happened back then, we generate a more profound effect and feel more fully what was happening with us in the past. Consider the following questions as if you are in the past right now.

- ❖ What is your first conversation with your man?
- ❖ What do you like about him the most?
- ❖ How does he make you feel?
- ❖ What makes you stay together?
- ❖ What do you share in common?

Visualise your partner as you remember seeing him those first few times. Is it the look in his eyes that is drawing you to him? Perhaps it is the tone of his voice or the strength of his hands. Maybe it is the conversations you shared.

Remember those times in your life when you were completely in love with him and he with you—the romance, the touch, and the way you looked at each other. See the image of those times. Feel it. Smell it. As a woman in love, I am crazy about my partner's voice, hands, and that wild look in his eyes.

What has happened since then to leave you feeling lost, cold, and somewhat alone?

To help you understand your current situation, I'd like you to imagine yourself entering a cold room. Inside, you find a tiny fire that has almost faded; the flames are struggling to stay alive. Amazingly, there is still some warmth there, and the embers are aglow. You have left it unattended, and now it is in danger of going out. You forgot how important heat is for cooking, staying warm, surviving, and dreaming. Gently blowing onto the fire, you place kindling in and around the warm coals. After a while your care is rewarded, and the fire begins to grow in vitality and force. Warm again, you jump up joyfully, celebrating your success by dancing around the fire, vowing to never neglect it again.

This fire is the relationship you have left unattended. Here is an opportunity to rekindle the flames of your love. Your relationship has incredible potential for the creation of deep intimacy and the flourishing of true love. You are no longer a teenager who doesn't really know how to love or how to give yourself to love. You are now an adult, who has experienced both pleasure and pain. *You* know!

The ability lies within you to create a new future that is bigger, stronger, deeper, and more passionate. Imagine how it would feel to know your man appreciates your erotic beauty and loves and adores you. How would it feel to see the spark of desire in his eyes? To know he sees you as the most gorgeous woman in his life? To be fulfilled by the depth of intimacy in your life?

Jo and Richard have been married for twenty-nine years. They have two grown children. Here is their story, as told by Jo, my client.

Our first session

> I don't know what's happening. I feel bored and stuck. We love each other; I know we love each other. And we feel comfortable with each other. But what is this longing? As if I'm missing something. You know, sex became so mechanical. I know exactly what's going to happen. It's booooring! How did we come to this place? I feel like I don't want to continue like this anymore. I want to feel excitement, passion. I want to enjoy making love with my husband. But it feels like that's it. We had our times and now everything is just plain boring. I don't want to live like that! It's killing me, this routine.

Our fifth session

> Well, I feel really good. You know, it seems like we are in love again. We touch each other more, and not just in a sexual way. We look at each other. I appreciate him a lot. And I feel warm and loved in his company. Last weekend we went away with our friends and stayed in a little cottage. I didn't want to make love because of the sound and closeness of our friends. So we just hugged, touched each other gently, while looking into each other's eyes. It was so delicious! I felt so connected to Richard. Then he

asked me if he could softly enter me, and I agreed. We lay there quietly, bathing in our love. It was so tender, so heart melting. We fell asleep like that.

Our ninth session

Our relationship is so good now. There is so much more depth there. You know, when we were young, we didn't have this amount of depth and intimacy. Now I feel confident in myself and secure in our relationship, and I am able to express the full range of my emotions. I'm able to express my love whenever I feel like it. I'm authentic, and I feel how I bring so much more depth—more of myself—to our relationship. And Richard feels so much stronger now. He is in control of his life and shows his feelings to me more easily. I see him as a separate, unique person now, not just my husband. I love who he has become. I never thought this could be possible. Our relationship is much better now than twenty-nine years ago. We trust each other, we respect each other, and we have more experience and wisdom. And sometimes we let it all go and play with each other as innocent kids. Yes, we have to nourish the relationship all the time and bring some excitement into it, but we have the resources and knowledge now.

This is what is possible. Are you ready to start our journey to deeper love? You can do this! Take comfort in the knowledge that you won't have to do it alone. I will walk with you along the path to the future of your desire and to deep fulfilling intimacy.

Create an Intention

Ask, and it shall be given you;
seek, and ye shall find;
knock, and it shall be opened unto you.
Matthew 7:7 King James 2000 Bible (©2003)

He who did not spare His own Son,
but delivered Him up for us all,
how will He not also with Him
freely give us all things?
Romans 8:32 King James 2000 Bible (©2003)

We need to let the universe know what we desire to create in our lives. Once we see the image of where we want to be and are able to articulate it, the universe has a chance to help us align our life with our vision. Once we know where we want to go, that vision draws us forward, and we see the reason for changing our habits. Our vision inspires us and keeps us moving forward, especially when our path seems littered with obstacles and progress feels slow.

Drawing a symbol that represents the future of our desires is a very potent tool to bring that future closer to us. A symbol brings in emotions and has an influence over our unconscious mind. Think of your country's national flag being raised at the Olympic Games—how proud and emotional we become. Or think of the importance of the wedding ring—how much it says to us about love and commitment. The more emotions we put into our intention, the stronger it becomes and therefore has more potency to manifest.

When I started to work on my relationship, this was my intention.

I create a playful, delicious, conscious, true partnership with my beloved, full of trust, openness, and intimacy. We support each other no matter what. I support, nurture, encourage, and care about my beloved. I inspire my beloved to manifest his highest potential. My beloved adores me. I feel supported and loved. I feel secure with him. Together we express and live the fullness of who we are. Our life is full of abundance. We live in joy and love. Everything is possible. Our life is full of adventure and growth.

Creating an Intention Practice

Close your eyes. Imagine the picture of your perfect relationship.

- ❖ How would you feel?
- ❖ What would you do together?
- ❖ How would you talk to each other?
- ❖ How would you look at each other?
- ❖ What would you see in his eyes?
- ❖ How would you want your partner to feel when he is with you?

See the vision of your dream relationship with all the details, colours, and smells. When you are ready, open your eyes and write your intention for your relationship in your journal.

Then draw a symbol for your desired relationship in your journal, or better yet, on a separate piece of paper. You can add your written intention there as well. Put this symbol somewhere visible. Read your intention daily to focus your mind on the vision you have and to send the signal of what you need into the universe so that it can be provided.

Remember, "Ask, and it shall be given."

Take Full Responsibility

I'm not in the mood for half-hearted
Mediocre is not enough
I never saw a half-hearted bird
Or a mediocre mountain
And every star in heaven
Has given its all
It's only me that's holding back
Suni

You can only change your relationship if you take full responsibility for it. Nothing else matters. If you are not prepared to be the master of your own life, you can put down my book right now. It won't work. If you take it on, let's conjure up some feminine magic together.

It is possible to create the relationship you've always wanted. This power is in your hands. Think about it; you can even create life! In ancient times a woman was revered as a goddess because she could create life. The role of men in procreation was unknown, and people believed women mysteriously created life inside their wombs. Women were revered as powerful and magical beings.

If we look around the ancient world, we will see there were plenty of goddesses in every culture, often with a very powerful divine mother goddess at the centre. Think of the legendary Aphrodite, who was the beautiful and seductive Greek goddess of love and beauty. Consider Gaia, ancient Earth Mother goddess, giver of life. In Greek mythology there was even a goddess of divine justice, order, and customs called Themis. In Egypt Ma'at was a goddess of truth, justice, and balance. She prevented creation from reverting to chaos, and she and her father judged the deeds of the dead. Another very powerful Egyptian goddess is Isis. She had an array of roles such as a fertility goddess and a goddess of magic and healing.

The role of the goddesses in Nordic mythology reflects the matriarchal society they came from. Women were considered to have natural psychic abilities and were acknowledged as shamans for their tribes. For example Freya was the Nordic goddess of love, beauty, fertility, war, wealth, and magic. Freya was known for her magnetic beauty, and no man could resist her when she wore her enchanting necklace.

Anywhere we go in the ancient world, we will encounter images of powerful women. They are our role models. Though they are not perfect moral figures, and some of them are subject to the destructive force of negative emotions. For example, Aphrodite suffered from insecurity and jealousy. While others, like Freya, sought to obtain what they desired, never taking into account the wants and needs of others. Nevertheless, these role models knew and owned their power. They didn't become victims of circumstance. They stood for what they desired.

You are a powerful, magnetic, and sensual woman. This is the life you cannot avoid: you were born in a woman's body. You were given the gift of creativity, and if you don't use it, there is a cost to the self. Most of us create our lives unconsciously, without any purpose, and then wonder why our life isn't the way we would ideally like it to be. If we don't use our creative power to develop love, connections with other people, and a sense of well-being, we will feel stuck, tense, like an old dried apple that missed its chance to provide nourishment.

> Louise is in her late thirties. She works as a travel agent, and when she isn't working, she is busy with

her two children. She is married to Tim. They've been together for the last fourteen years and seem to enjoy a peaceful marriage. But Louise feels that their life is too quiet. They do love each other, but life seems mechanical, and she misses the passion they had in the beginning. She misses the times when they kissed for hours on end and the times when being apart for one day seemed a horrifically long time. Now they say hi to each other when they get home from work and then get busy with their own lives. They go to bed at different times and have sex only once a week, in full darkness, and suppress all the sounds out of fear of waking their children. Sex follows the same route every time, and Louise does it to keep peace in the family. After Louise had several private sessions with me, Tim, her husband, shared the following with me:

"I'm amazed at how your work with my wife changed our relationship! I never experienced so much love and connection with my wife before, though we did love each other. But never before was our experience this deep. Never were we so open to each other and so intimate. Our sex life just went through the roof! I could never even imagine lovemaking as blissful and yummy. But I haven't changed, I think. How is this possible?"

This shows how much power women have to change their relationships. I know some women say their man needs to change first and do work on himself. But we are forgetting how powerful we are. It's much easier for us to connect to love and to attract our men into love. By nature women are more about love and connection; men are more about purpose and achieving. We are here to bring more love into life. I invite you to recognise your power and to start using it to create what you desire.

Blaming Doesn't Help

I often hear women blaming their partners, accusing them of unacceptable behaviour and a lack of consideration. Women don't realise that by blaming they imply their own powerlessness in the relationship. Ironically, that is probably what men would say too. It is like painting the ceiling in your house without covering the floor first, then wondering why the floor gets covered in paint drops—then blaming the paint.

It does not work to say:

- ❖ He needs to change.
- ❖ He needs to work on himself and open up to me. Then we can be happy.

You can try it, but I have yet to see it work. Men don't like to be the subject of our improvement projects. They resist and withdraw, retreating into the dark.

Look at your relationship. How often do you blame your partner? Maybe you blame him for not paying enough attention to you and not giving you what you need. Maybe you blame him because you feel bored in the relationship and feel a lack of excitement. Think back over the past week, and write down all the occurrences where you blamed him. I know it happens to me. Despite all I know about relationships, I still need to be aware and take full responsibility for my actions and my contributions to the relationship.

The truth is, if we blame we can't change anything. We go into victim mode and lose all our power. It is as if life happens to us, and we don't have any say in it. There is this nagging feeling that *it's not fair!*

It works to say:

- ❖ I take responsibility for what I'm unhappy about, and I stop blaming others.
- ❖ I work towards change, and I create the desired change in my life.

Discover How You Create Your Own Reality

I recently uncovered a pattern in my relationships with other people. Sometimes I feel that I am so different I can't connect to people and that some people will never understand me or appreciate me for who I am. Sometimes I feel judged by people who are different from me and even chopped down, the so called "tall poppy" syndrome.

I became curious about how I am contributing to this happening in my life. I noticed that when I meet people for the first time, I make judgements about who they are and how similar they are to me. If they are similar to me, I relax and open up to them. This promotes our connection even further; we talk and laugh and become friends. On the other hand, if the person I meet seems to be different from me, I become aloof, put my guard up, and don't show the softer, more vulnerable part of me. As a result this person doesn't have a chance to get to know me and is met by a ferocious warrior. No wonder he doesn't understand me and judges me as being cold and unfriendly.

This choice of my response to different people was not conscious. I became curious; what's the reason behind my selectiveness? I realised that it is fear of being hurt and not understood. My reaction out of this fear created the reality that proved that people who are not my tribe won't understand me and will judge me. And it's all my own creation! How powerful I am.

Now, I'm practicing staying open to different people and letting them into my inner world. It's amazing how kind and responsive people have become to me. Magic!

> Beverley was forty-nine years old, and she'd been married for nine years to Tony. She came to see me with the complaints that her relationship was falling apart, their communication was terrible, and she felt hopeless—nothing was working. We started to uncover how she created her own reality. Beverley told me she never felt loved. Moreover, she felt that she didn't deserve love because she was selfish and didn't have any love to give. When she came to this realisation, she broke down in tears. Beverley remembered coming home after being bullied at school. Her father was furious that her skirt was torn and dirty. He wouldn't listen to her explanations.
>
> "It's all your fault!" he said. "Why can't you be a good girl?"
>
> Beverley deduced from her father's attitude that she was wrong, she was bad, and she didn't deserve love. What a terrifying space for a little girl to be in. Beverley managed this terror by emotionally staying away from people in her little shell and judging other people as nasty and not deserving her attention.
>
> Once this underlying belief was uncovered, Beverly became conscious that she was the one who pushed her husband away. She didn't appreciate

Tony's efforts to make her happy and criticised him. She always questioned if he truly loved her and believed that he said nice things to her and bought presents because he wanted something of her, most often sex. Tony tried to prove to Beverly that he loved her, but finally he gave up. He was desolate to see that Beverly took his love as manipulation. He stopped trying. Beverley proved to herself that she didn't deserve love—she was right all along.

During our work Beverley got in touch with the truth of who she is: "I deserve love. I have so much love to give." She was able to receive love from her husband and appreciate him and his efforts to make her happy. Beverley turned her relationship around, enjoying a much deeper intimacy that she could ever possibly imagine.

Take a moment to consider what it is about your relationship that you are unhappy with. One example could be that your partner does not pay enough attention to you and is always busy with other things.

Ask yourself these questions.

- ❖ How am I contributing to him not paying enough attention to me?
- ❖ Do I do something to push him away?
- ❖ Do I act in a controlling way?
- ❖ Am I scared of him pulling away, which makes me so controlling it repels him?
- ❖ Am I spending a lot of time busy in my daily routines and not spending enough time sharing myself with my man thus pushing him away?

> ### A Note on Men
>
> A man wants to be romantic with a woman; he doesn't take his mate on a date.

Maybe you feel your partner doesn't appreciate you. Perhaps you think he should give you more attention and he is incapable of meeting your needs.

Ask yourself these questions.

- ❖ Do *you* appreciate yourself?
- ❖ Do *you* pay enough attention to yourself?
- ❖ Do *you* take care of yourself?
- ❖ Do you expect him to do what *you* are not doing for yourself?

People usually treat us the way we treat ourselves. If we do not appreciate and take care of ourselves, can we expect the men in our lives to behave differently?

To discover your own existential creativity, become curious about yourself and your way of being in your relationship. This is not achieved through judgement or blame. Just be curious. It is exciting and rewarding to reveal new things about the person we spend the most time with—ourselves.

Change the Way Your Man Treats You by Changing the Way You Treat Yourself

To start changing the way a man relates to a woman, she needs to change the way she treats herself. If you want your man to adore you, it is vital that first you adore yourself. If you want him to see you as an irresistible, sexy woman, you need to see yourself in the same light.

> Andrea, a forty-three-year-old woman came to me with the complaint that her partner didn't care about her pleasure and didn't satisfy her sexually. She was engaging in sex out of duty. She explained that sex was just not pleasurable for her, and she was not thrilled about the physical aspect of love. She gave her partner sex just to get him "off her back"; in fact Andrea resented him for taking her offer because, in her mind, he should have known she wasn't enjoying it.
>
> Meanwhile, when I talked to her partner, Bob, he said he knew Andrea was not enjoying sex. He wondered whether stopping sex altogether and giving up his pleasure would make their relationship better. He knew something needed to be changed, but he had no idea what.
>
> Bob's soul cried out: "If only she could tell me what I can do to make her happy! I feel like a failure. I can't even make my own wife happy. I'm clueless. Why can't we just live in love and harmony?"
>
> According to Andrea it was Bob's fault that she could not be satisfied sexually.
>
> I asked her these questions: "Do you know how to satisfy yourself? Do you share with Bob what

makes you feel excited and hungry for more? Do you know your pleasure anatomy?"

Andrea looked at me in disbelief as if I had said something heretical. She said, "But he is a man! He is supposed to know!" And then she laughed and laughed at the absurdity of her assumption.

> **Treat Yourself the Way You Want Your Man to Treat You Practice**
>
> 1. In your journal make a list of experiences and feelings you want from your man.
> 2. Find a way to provide these experiences and feelings to yourself. Use your imagination to design a way to give yourself the love, attention, understanding, and care you desire from your man.

SECRETS OF WEEK 1

1. Remember the love and passion you had in the beginning.
2. Create an intention to let the universe know what you desire.
3. Take full responsibility for where you are in your life.
4. Recognise that women are powerful and magical beings.

5. Stop blaming others for what is happening in your life. It takes your power away.
6. Discover how you create your own reality.
7. Change the way your man treats you by changing the way you treat yourself.

Practice Week 1

Take Full Responsibility

Decide—right now—that you have the power to change your relationship. For this practice you will need to speak your responses out loud with intensity and passion. Breathe deeply. Move your body and feel your power arising from deep inside you.

You need to use your whole body, your voice, and your emotions to plant this new idea of how powerful you are deep within your psyche. Then every time you notice a pull back towards feeling helpless, your mind and your body will remind you what it costs to feel helpless and that it is completely up to you to change your relationship.

Consider the following questions and write your answers in your journal. Then say the answers out loud with passion and intensity.

1. What has it cost me to not take full responsibility and to feel helpless?
2. Who has it hurt and how badly?
3. How has it hurt me?
4. What do I lose when I feel helpless and blame others?

After that claim your power by saying out loud:

"I'm powerful. I can create life. I can create the relationship I desire. The power is in my hands."

Do this practice every day for at least five minutes for the next week. Be committed to it. Put all your passion into this practice to rewire your brain. At first you might have doubts and might struggle to feel your power in your body. Nevertheless, continue this practice every day. You will notice how your attitude changes. You will start to feel the power and determination in your body, your thoughts, and your emotions.

For me when the thought *I cannot do this, no one wants me* enters my mind, something inside me raises its head, taking a warrior stance and proclaiming strongly:

"No! This is not true! My life is in my hands. I am powerful! I have the ability to create what I want!"

Automatically, my shoulders relax and go back. As if by miracle I become five centimetres taller. Yessss!!!

Homeplay Week 1

Give to Yourself

What is that you want to receive from your partner? Make a date with yourself and provide this experience for yourself. Maybe you need to listen to your feelings, appreciate your beauty, or take yourself for a walk.

WEEK 2

The Most Powerful Way to Turn Your Relationship Around—Ready? Jump!

> *The biggest disease today is not leprosy or tuberculosis, but rather the feeling of being unwanted, uncared for and deserted by everybody.*
> Mother Teresa

Get Clear on the Negative Patterns in Your Relationship

If you are still reading this, it means that you recognise your power and are ready to turn your relationship around. Hooray for you! Let's continue on this journey together.

The next step is to change the frustrating patterns that can occur in our relationships. Can you think of something, perhaps even a small thing, which happens again and again between you and your partner that continually frustrates you?

Here is the story of one of my clients.

> At the time, Anna and her husband, Oleg, were in their mid-thirties. They used to run a tourism business together. Oleg would sometimes tell Anna that he wanted her to communicate with their clients with more warmth and care or that he would prefer her to dress differently when meeting tourists at the airport. Anna would react and say that nothing was ever good enough for him, and they would often argue. Eventually, Oleg stopped asking Anna to change her ways. With time tourists no longer joined their tours as they could feel that this was not a happy, relaxed tour company. Eventually, Oleg sold the business. Rather than admit their tour company was a complete disaster, they told everyone they needed a change and had decided to start breeding quails.
>
> Anna became my client once the tension in the relationship was such that their new business was suffering from the same stress as the previous one. In addition their home life was no longer as passionate and joyful as the couple had hoped for when they got married.
>
> What had really happened to their marriage? Every time Oleg suggested a way to improve their business, Anna went into her pattern of believing

that she must not be good enough and no one would ever love her.

She was reacting to his suggestions at home, too. One time he told me how he had suggested that she buy some sexy lingerie for herself. He thought, *Wow, you'd look really hot in it! I'd love to see the wild, sexy side of you.* But her interpretation was that he no longer desired her, and that his intention was to turn her into someone else.

Her way of dealing with her hopelessness was to attack him for making her feel unworthy and rejected. She wasn't open to considering her husband's suggestions because she believed he was actually criticising her and telling her that she was not good enough. After Oleg was on the receiving end of several outbursts of her emotions, he stopped making suggestions to improve their business and relationship. He gave up on his business dream and decided to keep the peace in the family by withdrawing some of his energy from the relationship.

Anna's inability to hear any criticism or negative feelings destroyed the intimacy between them. To avoid any further drama Oleg stayed only halfway in the relationship. Without being able to talk openly about negative feelings, they stopped having fun, and their passion dried up. When they came to see me, they were discussing letting the quails fly free, selling their house, and renting two separate apartments.

What do you think this couple could have done to re-ignite their love?

I learned about an interesting anger-versus-passion pattern from working with many different people. What usually happens first is that couples start to see their anger and frustration as negative feelings. This comes about because they notice how the other partner reacts, and they want to avoid hurting the person they love; or perhaps they simply want to keep the peace and avoid the constant drama.

However, anger and frustration are very human emotions. Once couples cut off from their anger and stop expressing their frustrations to their partner, they have to hide that part of themselves, guarding against those emotions.

Let's be honest—it is impossible to not get angry or frustrated sometimes. When that so called "negative" part is pushed to one side, partners withhold a part of themselves from the relationship and are not fully engaged. This keeps them restricted, in a sense, and short of breath. As a result the passion in the relationship dies out.

This does not mean that we should scream and throw dishes at each other. We need to find a way to express our "negative" emotions in a safe way—perhaps beating a pillow, screaming your heart out on the beach, or doing an intense workout. Then we are ready to express ourselves without the heated emotional charge. We also need to allow our partners to express their feelings without reacting to them and taking those expressed emotions personally.

How I Discovered My Goddess Truth

When my partner goes through his moon cycle (yes, men also have their cycles, though most of them are not tuned in to them), he is less interested in physical intimacy and disconnects from me. Instead, he focuses on work and himself. This turning of his focus away from me used to make me feel unwanted. Eventually, I became curious and questioned when precisely this feeling had first come into my life. I realised it was when I was little girl and I was left home alone. It was a universal Russian condition: parents had to work full time, and children were left home by themselves from a very young age.

This is the reason, when my beloved disconnects from me, I tend to go straight into my childhood feelings of abandonment. I might feel angry for being abandoned or feel sad and unworthy of attention. I start to think that my partner doesn't care about me, doesn't want me, and doesn't love me. And I begin thinking that I'm going to break up with him because *I deserve something better!* What this means, in fact, is that I am afraid he will leave me. I would prefer to leave him first to keep myself safe and to stay in control.

When our acts stem from our negative judgements, we re-create the same situation to prove to ourselves that we were right. If I were to continue to react to my partner from this "hurt-little-girl" space, I would be projecting my past and my childhood onto him. I would be recreating to what happened in the past. He would have no idea why I was angry at him. It would be unreasonable to expect him to be attracted to me and spend time with me when I'm in a "hurt-little-girl" space. That will only serve to make him disconnect from me even further and put his shutters down.

As a result even though my own withdrawal caused the situation, I will believe that I have proved to myself that never ever will anyone want me and love me for who I am. I just can't trust anyone!

Notice that "never ever." This is usually a sign that our little girl is speaking—she's dramatic and unable to see the whole picture. She is unreasonable, has little patience, and feels every disappointment or rejection as she would a physical stake to the heart. Imagine a three-year-old pouting when she is not allowed to put a summer dress on when it's snowing outside and you get the picture.

Using the process that I will take you through in the practice section for this week, an amazing shift happened in my life. I discovered my *goddess truth*. Now I can physically feel the difference within my body and can truly know that:

- ❖ Life supports me
- ❖ I am wanted by all of life
- ❖ I am a blessing to life
- ❖ I am a blessing to other people
- ❖ People who are aligned with my values are craving for me to share my gifts
- ❖ I choose to be a force of love and joy on this planet
- ❖ My beloved deeply appreciates and loves me
- ❖ We are here together to create more joy and love, to give full expression to our potential, and to live in our full loving power

When I slip back into my old beliefs, thinking *I'm not wanted* or *I'm a mistake*, and start to feel stressed and depressed, I remember my reality, my deeper *goddess truth*. And I choose to live in full bloom.

Who am I? Ah, yes! I'm a blessing to life! I choose to be the force of love and joy! So what do I do now? I choose to see myself for precisely who I am. I recognise that life supports me, and I celebrate life. I share my love and joy with other people. How can I stay stressed and depressed when I remember my truth!

Now, when my man needs time by himself, I catch myself getting hurt and jumping into my "little-girl-space." I remember my *goddess truth*, and as a result I stay open and loving to my partner with a knowledge that he does care about me. That deep inside he wants to make me happy. Then as soon as he is out of his private retreat, I welcome him back with a smile and an attitude of acceptance. Our connection is restored. And what I notice now is that he comes back to me much faster because he feels my loving presence and doesn't want to miss out on the fun and intimacy we share.

A Note on Men

Here is a huge secret for you about men. Men need time on their own. They need to do their manly activities. They need time with other men just as we need time with other women. When a man goes away to do his own thing, it has nothing to do with the woman in his life and is not a reflection on how he feels about her. Sometimes he might stay home but will need to disconnect emotionally from his partner. A woman shouldn't be alarmed and definitely shouldn't try to reconnect with him by talking to him and following him. That will irritate a man and push him away.

Instead, if she continues to do what makes her happy and stays open and loving towards her man, he'll come back to her much sooner and will want to spend time with his beloved.

I can't stress this enough: try to not take his behaviour personally! Remember, that men are not multi-focused. When they are involved in something, they simply cannot keep us uppermost in their minds. Men always need to stay focused on the task at hand. This is how they are able to achieve their goals, catch that deer, and move forward. It is primal, the hunter in them. Their ability to focus is a gift!

SECRETS OF WEEK 2

1. Get clear on the negative patterns that occur in your relationship.
2. Acknowledge that we all need to be able to express our negativity towards our partners in order to keep the passion present in the relationship.
3. Learn how to express your anger without damaging your relationship, for example, by beating a pillow, screaming on the beach, or going for an intense workout.
4. Express your negative feelings to your partner after the emotional charge is released in non-damaging ways.
5. Allow the space for your partner to express his negative feelings towards you without taking them personally.
6. Catch yourself reacting to your partner and jumping straight into your "hurt-little-girl" state.
7. Discover your inner *goddess truth* and respond to your partner from this empowered state.

Practice Week 2

I'm safe in the Universe. All of life loves and supports me.
Louise Hay

Discovering Your Goddess Truth Practice

The following process is an adaptation of my work with "Feminine Power" led by Claire Zammit and Katherine Woodward Thomas, Anthony Robbins therapist training, the work of Byron Katie and Osho based therapies.

Have your journal nearby to record your insights.

First, read through this practice.

Then please go to www.deeplyinloveagain.com/bookpractice and download the recording that I made especially for you. In the recording I will take you through this practice to allow you to drop deeper into yourself and discover your *goddess truth* without having to focus on reading. This is the foundational practice, so I strongly encourage you to listen to the recording and do this practice before moving to the next chapter.

This is the moment to remember the most recent instance when negative tension was apparent in your relationship. Close your eyes and remember this event in every detail.

- ❖ Where were you?
- ❖ What did you say or not say?
- ❖ What did he say or not say?

Imagine that it just happened again. Feel it in your body. Breathe.

- ❖ How do you feel?
- ❖ What happens inside you?

Name your feelings without judging them or trying to change anything. Welcome these feelings. Become curious: *Oh, that's what I feel! How interesting! What else?*

Turn your attention towards, not away from, these uncomfortable feelings.

Then explore the following.

- ❖ Where in your body do you feel your frustration, irritation, anger, sadness, helplessness, or whatever feeling you struggle with?
- ❖ What colour is it?
- ❖ How dense is it?
- ❖ How big is it? Is it the size of a pea, or does it fill your whole body—maybe even the whole room?
- ❖ How old is this feeling?
- ❖ When did I first experience it?"

Let the answers arise as you simply wait for them.

Quite often this same feeling goes back to childhood, to a time when our parents weren't their perfect selves and didn't respond lovingly and patiently to our needs.

Open your eyes. Stay connected to the emotions triggered by your partner's behaviour. Ask yourself the following questions and write the answers in your journal.

1. What did I think of my partner when this event happened?
2. What did I think of myself when this event happened?
3. What did I think of life when this event happened?

Write whatever comes to your mind, even if it doesn't make sense or doesn't sound nice and elegant. Let your hand write and your feelings be expressed without judging or censoring yourself.

How do you feel when you believe these thoughts about your partner, yourself, and life? Write your answer.

Now, stand up and do a little dance, shake your emotions off. Lift your head, look out your window at the sky, and take a deep breath. (For some reason, it's difficult to be negative and depressed when physically looking up. Usually, to feel sad and depressed, we need to look down).

Have a look at your notes now. Are the thoughts you wrote in your journal about yourself, your partner, and life true? Question yourself and your beliefs. Do a reality check. Are your judgements completely true? If you answered yes, ask yourself the next question: are they absolutely 100 percent true?

Next, remember a moment when you were head over heels in love with your man. A time when you were so happy about yourself and who you were that life seemed utterly wonderful.

Ah, I love you! Ah, I love my life! Ah, I feel so good about myself!

Feel grateful for what you have, for your beautiful relationship, and for the man who is such an important part of your life.

From this place of gratitude and joy, ask yourself, "What is true?"

- ❖ Who am I, really?
- ❖ What is my deeper truth?
- ❖ What is the purpose of my life?
- ❖ Who is my man for me?
- ❖ What is life for me?

Create short statements for what is true, and write them in your journal. Create statements that contradict your original negative beliefs and cancel them out. I call these statements your inner *goddess truth*. Once you find the statements that click, you will feel a shift in your body, a sense of expansion, and maybe some emotional release like laughter, shaking, or tears.

Perhaps it is:

- ❖ I am a sensual, sexy woman.
- ❖ I embody love and beauty.
- ❖ I deserve love because I have so much love to give.
- ❖ I am here to give and receive love.
- ❖ I am a desirable woman.
- ❖ I'm more than enough. I have so much to offer to my man and other people.

- ❖ I deeply love my partner even though sometimes he upsets me.
- ❖ My partner supports me and wants to make me happy.
- ❖ I love my man and want to make him happy and share my love with him.
- ❖ I respect and care for my partner even though we have different views on life.
- ❖ I love and honour the spark of the divine in my partner.
- ❖ Life supports me and wants me to be here.
- ❖ Life needs my contribution.
- ❖ I'm safe in the universe. All of life loves and supports me.

Find your truth that doesn't depend on your current circumstances or what is happening in your relationship right now. Become your own sovereign. Write the statements in your journal and memorise them.

If you still have traces of your negative judgements in your head, imagine they rapidly evaporate and disappear with the clouds. How do you feel when you read your *goddess truth* and completely believe it? If you need to, imagine that you believe it, that this is the only truth.

Pick up your brushes or pencils, and paint a symbol that represents your *goddess truth*. Seeing it every day will empower you and leave an imprint in your mind. It has the potential to transform your life.

How to Apply This Practice in Your Relationship

Now every time you start feeling uneasy or irritated or unloved in your relationship, become curious about what you feel, open up to your feelings, and accept them. Listen to your inner hurt little girl and accept and welcome her feelings. Talk to yourself as you would to your child who comes to you and says, "No one loves me. I am bad. I am wrong. No one wants me to be here."

Become a nurturing fearless mother to your inner child—a mother who stands for the truth and supports and protects her child. Affirm to your "little girl" the truth of who she really is. It's not that she is not enough and doesn't deserve love, it's that her parents were not perfect, or perhaps they were self-absorbed or had to work a lot to earn a living. It's not that the world is not a safe place, but that her father couldn't manage his aggression in an appropriate way. It's not that she's not wanted by people and life, but that her mother was too young, scared, and ashamed for becoming pregnant. Let her know the truth. *Life wants you, life loves and supports you! You are safe in the universe! Because I love you. I want you. I support you. I bless you.*

Once you reaffirm your *goddess truth* to yourself, you will shift from the "hurt-little-girl" state to the powerful woman state. Act from the place of your truth rather than from a place that makes you form negative judgements of your man, yourself, and life.

Homeplay Week 2

1. Waking up Your Sensual Woman

Wear a long skirt, and take off your underwear to feel the wind and be free. Go for a walk on the beach or in the forest.

2. Activating the Connection Between Your Sex and Heart Centres

Feel your yoni (Tantra word for female genitals), your sexual centre and the seat of your pleasure. Feel your heart centre in the middle of your chest, the seat of your love. Imagine that you have a channel extending from your yoni into your heart. Breathe in from your yoni up the channel and into your heart. Breathe out from your heart into your yoni. Feel these two beautiful centres connecting, uniting your pleasure and your love.

WEEK 3

Let's Fill Up Your Love Tanks!

How can a need be love? Love is a luxury. It is abundance. It is having so much life that you don't know what to do with it, so you share. It is having so many songs in your heart that you have to sing them—whether anybody listens is not relevant.
Osho

Love From an Overflow

Love is all about sharing and giving from an overflow, a place of abundance. Love is not about trying to make our man give us what we missed in our childhood and what we are missing now. The simple truth here is, we are fully capable of giving ourselves what we need. It's a marvellous thing to share our joy and love of life with our man. To be partners in the adventures of life. To make mischief together. To celebrate our beauty. To celebrate his beauty. To have delicious, ecstatic sex.

Please, please don't use your beloved to make you feel better when you feel bad. Don't use him for security or as a wall between you and life. Don't use him as an object you own or as someone who has to read your mind and make you happy. We tend to overburden our intimate relationships with demands and expectations. We forget that it takes a village to raise a child and the whole world to keep us happy and alive. Don't demand that your partner vanquish your existential aloneness. It is your spirit calling you to realise your full potential and live your wholeness.

A man can't possibly fulfil all the roles assigned to him nowadays. He is expected to earn a good living to provide for his family. He is expected to help with the housework. He is expected to listen to his woman and understand her needs. He is expected to be always emotionally available and at the same time to be a sexy, strong alpha male. It gets to be too much, and sometimes all he can do to manage the pressure is retreat into darkness. It's the same way a modern woman is expected to work and achieve in her career, to be a housewife who keeps the house clean and guest-ready, to be a nurturing mum who gives birth effortlessly and raises well-behaved children, and to be a passionate sex expert in bed. We expect way too much of ourselves nowadays.

We need to start prioritising and creating support structures that remove the unnecessary pressures from our intimate relationships. Relationships are for pleasure. If there is no pleasure in a relationship, then something needs to change.

For a woman to enjoy her man, she needs to have her love tanks full before she meets him. Of course, sometimes it's nice to moan about how unfair life is and let him prove to her that she is beautiful and smart and worthy of all the flowers, but this can't be the basis for a harmonious loving relationship. It is just plain unfair to him. We need to start taking responsibility for ourselves and start practicing extreme self-care. It's not selfish to take care of oneself. It's absolutely necessary. Because if we don't replenish ourselves, there will nothing left to give. Because if we just give to others and take care of others without refilling ourselves, we will become resentful of those to whom we give.

Uncover Your Co-dependency Patterns

Reflect on the following questions.

- ❖ When was the last time you refuelled yourself with love and uplifting experiences?
- ❖ When was the last time you sacrificed your well-being for others?
- ❖ When you provide care for others, what belief or emotion is the driving force?
- ❖ When you sacrifice your well-being, what belief or emotion is the driving force?
- ❖ Are these beliefs or emotions really true?

I love running and practicing yoga on the beach. It fulfils me, awakens my sensuality, and gives me so much joy. Some days I decide that work is more important—that I'm not moving forward fast enough, and I need to be more focused and disciplined. By the end of such a day, I become exhausted, unmotivated, and unsure of why I'm even doing what I'm doing. This is the result of prioritising my achievements over my physical and emotional well-being. Then I realise—I need to practice extreme self-care. I need to support myself to flourish, and then my work will flourish and serve so many more people. Who needs an unhappy and stressed reignite-your-love coach?

What recently surfaced in my conscious mind is the belief that I can't take care of myself. In my logical mind, of course, I know I can, but my inner little girl still looks for a parent. I realised that's why sometimes I struggle with taking care of myself. It comes out of a belief that someone else should come along and make sure I'm okay, fed, and happy. Once I got curious about this belief, I discovered that sometimes I interact with people as if asking a question "Am I okay? Do you like me? Will you take care of me?" This is a co-dependency pattern—the need to make others like me so they make me feel safe and take care of me. To transform my relationship with myself and others, I talk to my little girl. I ask her how she feels and what she needs. And I let her know that I'm here to take care of her, that we don't need anyone else. I choose to practice extreme self-care, provide myself with what I need, and stop my co-dependency pattern.

Become curious and find out if you have a hidden question when you interact with people. What drives your social conversations, your verbal and nonverbal exchanges with your man, and your desire to care for others? Is it the yearning to authentically connect with and contribute to other people? Or are you motivated by fear and therefore try to control your environment by making sure people like and need you?

I invite you to take a stand for your life and practice extreme self-care. What makes your eyes shine? What fulfils you and makes the stars fall out of your heart and onto every passerby?

Seven Fundamentals to Keep Us Happy

*The world needs your flame—but first,
you need the oil for your lamp.*
Lisa Hammond

There are seven fundamentals that are vital for women to fully enjoy life (Again this number. Though I'm sure you can come up with more. Let me know what I've missed).

1. Movement

Human beings in general thrive on movement, and women especially need movement to feel sensual.

What does it mean to be sensual? It means to be in contact with our feelings and sensations. Awakening our senses can greatly enhance our total life experience to its maximum potential. We women can be lusciously sensual. We have the capacity to experience oodles of pleasure. So much fullness of life.

To connect to our bodies, we need movement that brings us joy. Are you dancing or practicing any other kind of movement that makes you feel excited and ready to jump out of bed? Think of movement rather than exercise. The thought of exercise can be draining and that's the opposite of what we need.

As you probably know, movement increases our happiness hormones and brings vitality and health to our bodies. Now think of an extra benefit—enhancing your love-making! Don't you want to just whirl into dancing straight away? I strongly encourage you to make space and time for movement every day.

2. Healthy Diet

Yes, Beautiful, yes. Healthy eating is important for love.

How is your diet? Sometimes nutritionists make it rather hard. In fact it's pretty simple. Eat more raw greens, colourful veggies, and fruits. Buy as little as possible packaged food, and drink lots of pure water. Homemade food prepared with love and joy can do miracles. Start eating more fruits and sweet root vegetables, and you will have fewer cravings for sweets.

The way we eat is also important. We need to take our time, make sure we are relaxed and calm before eating, and chew our food thoroughly. If we chew more, we get more nourishment from our food, and as a result we eat less. Digestion actually begins in the mouth, where contact with our teeth and the digestive enzymes in our saliva break down food. But quite often we rush through the whole eating experience, barely acknowledging what we're putting it in our mouths. We often are distracted or in a hurry when we eat, so we swallow our food practically whole. This inattentiveness to food creates a host of digestive problems and leads to becoming overweight.

As I've learnt from my studies at the Institute for Integrative Nutrition, there are many great reasons to slow down and chew our food.

- ❖ Saliva breaks down food into simple sugars, creating a sweet taste. The more we chew, the sweeter our food becomes, so we don't crave those after-meal sweets.
- ❖ Chewing reduces digestive distress and improves assimilation, allowing our bodies to absorb maximum nutrition from each bite of food.

- ❖ More chewing produces more endorphins, the brain chemicals responsible for creating good feelings.
- ❖ It's also helpful for weight loss, because when we are chewing well, we are more apt to notice when we are full.
- ❖ In fact chewing can promote increased circulation, enhanced immunity, and increased energy and endurance, and it can improve skin health and stabilise weight.
- ❖ Taking time with a meal, beginning with chewing, allows for enjoyment of the whole experience of eating: the smells, flavours and textures. It helps us become more aware and sensual.

I remember having mango parties where we embarked on eating mangoes as sensually as possible. My whole body awoke from slowly and gracefully savouring these juicy sweet fruits. An erotic experience! I can imagine that is the way goddesses are relishing their heavenly feasts.

Try eating slowly and attentively without any distractions, focusing on food and chewing. This is a great practice to slow down and awaken your senses, which will be very useful once we get to week six and start experimenting with slow and connected lovemaking.

Many of us restrict food, attempting to control our weight. We often abuse food, substituting it for emotional well-being. Others ignore food, swallowing it whole before they've even tasted it. What would our life be like if we treated food and our body as we would treat our beloved—with gentleness, playfulness, communication, honesty, respect, and love?

I invite you to become curious about your relationship with food, and start treating your body with love and respect, as if you are feeding your baby. Of course you want to feed your baby the most nutritious food.

3. Sleep

We need rest. Sleep is so essential for us to feel sexy and loving. Don't underestimate its significance. They say that for our biological clock to be at its best, we need to go to sleep by ten at night and get up by seven in the morning. This makes us feel thrilled about the new day and more inclined to share our love with our man. Do you feel loving and sexy when you are tired? Make it a habit to go to bed by ten to enjoy your dreams.

Sleep is far from a waste of time. It recharges our batteries, fills us up with patience and love, and allows our spirits to process each day's events in a gentle manner.

4. Spending Time with Girlfriends

It's amazing what the company of women can do for us. Have you tried a girls' weekend away? It can do wonders. We nourish each other, and we fill each other with sensual, calm, and nurturing energy. Finally, talking about our feelings without someone else, trying to solve the problem. What a miracle. Girlfriends are the best people to unload our "stuff" with. They listen. They know we just need to talk and empty our heads. After we are nourished and cleansed, we have much more capacity to meet our man and be ready for romance.

Do a favour for yourself—spend at least one day a week with your girlfriends, sharing your feelings, your hopes, your desires, being a woman with women. In traditional societies it used to be a very important part of a woman's life. I believe we need to make an effort to be with other women, support other women, and receive support from them. Allow the beauty of being with women come into your life.

My client Beatrix was working in a male-dominated environment, and she had two sons. She was surrounded by men. And she didn't have close relationship with women in her life. She came to see me and was complaining that there is no romance in her relationship. She and her husband were more like buddies, and he stopped treating her as a woman. No gifts, no compliments, and no special time together.

I saw a lot of masculine energy in her. Her whole posture and way of communicating was more like that of a man than of a woman. She was direct, to the point, very goal oriented, and she had forgotten how to giggle and flirt with men. But she definitely knew what she wanted and was very determined to achieve it.

Women are very adaptable. That has been our way of surviving since time immemorial. Beatrix was spending most of her time in male company, and she adapted her behaviour to mimic that of a man. This made communicating with men much easier. However, the sexual attraction with her husband disappeared, and Beatrix ended up feeling lost and drained.

One of the suggestions I made to her was that she spend more time with women and make a conscious effort to connect and open herself up to other women. Once she received nurturing from other women, she noticeably relaxed and started to send electric smiles to her husband and behave more as a woman. Interestingly enough, he became more attracted to her and even brought her flowers one day. Beatrix was thrilled! There was more work to be done, but the basis for transformation was already there.

5. Time Alone and Spiritual Practice

How do you feel after spending time by yourself? With our busy lifestyles, we often forget how good it feels to spend time alone and connect with ourselves.

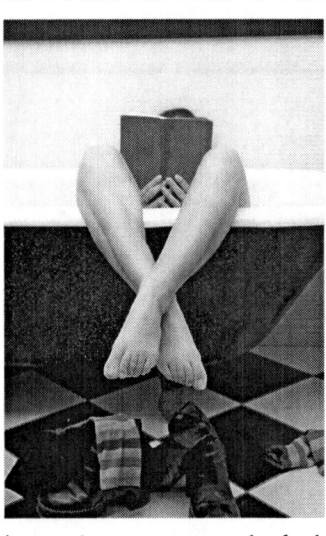

We need to have alone time to centre ourselves and check what's happening inside. We need time to distance ourselves from our life's everyday issues. We need time to see the bigger picture, to plug into the energy of the universe, and to sense the higher purpose of our lives.

Spending time with nature can be your spiritual practice. Meditating and stepping out of my mind, becoming an unattached observer, is an essential practice for me. Maybe you prefer to dance or paint as your spiritual practice. The main properties of spiritual practice are regularity, stillness of mind, and connection to higher energies to experience a deeper purpose of our life here.

My practice is swimming in the ocean every morning. I make a ritual out of it. Before going into the water, I say what I'm grateful for and then ask for what I want. Sometimes I ask for more love in my heart or fearless actions or clarity of my purpose. After the swim I stand barefoot on the beach and feel the connection to the earth and sky. I feel the energy of the universe running through me and pronounce my intention for the day. In this way I feel like I'm living my higher purpose, fully engaged with life and expressing my full potential.

6. Time with Nature

I love hugging trees. It's an uplifting experience. Have you tried hugging a tree? Going for a walk on the beach or in forest is very nourishing. As women we are more connected to nature and mother earth. We need to spend time in nature to nurture that connection. It is important for our physical and spiritual well-being. Fresh air heals our bodies, purifies us, and gives us so much energy. The sun energises us, increases our happiness hormones, and supplies our bodies with important vitamin D. The wind blows out destructive thoughts and wakes up the sensuality of our skin. Have you done the homeplay practice from week two? Try it again—going for a walk in a long skirt without your knickers. Just you and the glorious feeling of the wind on your skin.

7. Sensual Touch and Sex

Sensory stimulation is a nutrient that the brain must have to develop and function normally.
James Prescott

Don't you love to be touched? Without any agenda or plans for sex, just enjoying human hands on your skin? Ah, it's so wonderful! I love full body massages; I feel all of my body, every single part of it pulsing with life and pleasure.

Make a "touching date" with your man. It's better to agree that you won't go into sex. Just caress each other, feeling the skin and awakening your senses. Choose whose turn is first to receive and indulge in the feelings without trying to give your touch and love at the same time. Be totally selfish! Then when it's your turn to give, fully give and enjoy giving. If you touch each other at the same time, it diffuses the intensity and doesn't give so much pleasure. Try to be in a completely giving or receiving mode. This can feel very vulnerable and exciting . . . so explore!

We need sex. It's not just about pleasure; it's important for our well-being and full enjoyment of life. Have as much sex as you can fit into your busy lifestyle, and make it more important than going to the gym. This is your most important workout. Take it seriously—scheduling your dates—and have as much wild fun or soft melting intimacy as your system can take. But it needs to be the way you like it. I'll share more with you on maximising your sexual pleasure in weeks six and seven.

In the next section I will talk about giving sensual pleasure and touch to ourselves. It's good to remember to give ourselves what we want our man to give to us.

Self-Cultivation: Discover Your Pleasure Anatomy

Self-cultivation is an ancient Chinese Tao practice, meaning the art of self-pleasuring. The idea is that we have to become our own best lovers and cultivate our own sexual energy before we can be really fulfilled in sexual interactions with others.

Think about it: if we don't know what brings us pleasure, how is a man supposed to know what to do and how to touch us? We assume that they should know. But where would they learn it? They probably spent time with women who didn't really tell them what to do and just went along with whatever was happening. Do we know the most exciting way to touch our man and pleasure him? Wouldn't it be nice if he tells us exactly what he likes and desires so we don't have to grope in the darkness hoping that we are doing ok?

Do you know our clitoris is as extensive and powerful organ as the penis, consists of eighteen parts, and is even similar in size to the penis, just inside of our bodies? I suggest reading *The Clitoral Truth* by Rebecca Chalker to fully understand our anatomy.

We need to know our bodies and then teach our partners how to give us the most exquisite pleasure. In her book, Chalker writes:

> At least we know the clitoral truth: that women have a complex and powerful genital system that is designed for one specific purpose—*pleasure*. This knowledge should encourage us to explore our capacity for sexual response, and help us to do it with confidence and assurance.

Take a moment to contemplate self-cultivation. I like this word much better than masturbation, which is a bit rough and sometimes has a negative connotation. It can be an amazing adventure exploring our own sexuality, sometimes filled with joy and sometimes with pain and frustration. But the more hidden secrets of our body and psyche we discover, the more open and sensuous we become, and the more enjoyable sex becomes. I am speaking from my own direct experience.

I remember when I was seventeen and had my first sexual experience. The desire was so strong, but the actual experience was quite disappointing. At that time I felt that the whole experience of lovemaking was mechanical, animal-like, and it didn't really satisfy my desire. But how could my boyfriend at the time figure out what I wanted even if I didn't know what made me tick? At that time I realised that I had a lot of judgements about sex but didn't really know my physical and emotional self.

Since then I have made a point to explore my sexuality and find out what excites me, what brings out deep emotions in me, and what kind of touch I prefer.

Self-cultivation helped me to enhance my sensuality and overcome some of my deep-seated shame around sexuality. Sex wasn't a subject that was discussed in my family, so I unconsciously regarded it as something that needs to be done in the dark, hidden away from everyone. It was something to be ashamed of. Something that "good girls" don't do, or at least don't enjoy doing.

The importance of masturbation is really to love and care for yourself totally, as a natural way of relating to your own body. It is a normal activity that would logically be a part of any woman's life.
Shere Hite

Self-Cultivation Practice

I find it helps to put a bit of structure into making the experience deep and meaningful.

As usual it's important to have some uninterrupted time and to create an intimate ambience.

Then, think of your intention for your self-cultivation session. What would you like to experience or find out or overcome? Say your intention out loud to make it real.

The orgasm is not the goal. It's about your connection to yourself and the exploration of your body. You don't even have to touch your genitals if it's daunting for you. There is a lot to explore there, but only when you are ready.

Next, start touching yourself in a conscious, loving, and very present way, just as you would like your perfect lover to touch you. Become that perfect lover for yourself. Go slowly and explore all the little corners of your body, making sure you pay attention to all of your body and spreading your gorgeous sexual energy all around you. Feel how beautiful loving yourself is! How could anyone ever tell you otherwise?!

At the end hug yourself, talk to yourself sweetly, and when you are ready, reflect on your intention and what happened during the session. Write your reflections in your journal for deeper insights.

Practice self-cultivation every day for a week to get connected to your sexual energy. After that it's a good habit to practice self-cultivation at least once a week.

> For one of your sessions, you might want to use your mirror. Look at yourself during the session—see your beautiful body and gaze deeply into your eyes. You will see yourself without any persona, just the way your lover sees you. Stay deeply engaged with yourself regardless of what happens. Just as you would like your perfect lover to stay present with you no matter what emotional turmoil or ecstatic pleasure you are going through.
>
> I was quite taken by one of my mirror sessions. I was looking in my eyes and saw so much beauty. It made me realise for the first time why someone might be in love with me. Of course, so much beauty! So precious and vulnerable. I fell in love with myself and couldn't stop gazing into my own eyes. And the amazing thing, whenever I moved my eyes, I was still looking directly into my eyes. I was crying and smiling and telling snow loads of beautiful things to myself.

Benefits of Self-Cultivation

Here is what my client Diane says about the benefits of self-pleasuring.

> It is an act of self-love for me. At times when I focus on self-pleasuring, I don't feel need in other people. I fulfil myself. I used to be so needy of love, so dependent on my lover that I would push him away with my neediness. Now, I'm my own best lover. It keeps my erotic energy flowing. And this makes me so much more attractive to my partner.

Previously, I used to masturbate in a certain way, without being conscious of myself and locked in the fantasy. Now, it's like a meditation practice for me, time to be with myself, feel the energy running through my body. It is very centring and grounding. If I self-pleasure in the morning, I have good energy for the day. Self-pleasuring was a big part for me for releasing shame around my sexuality. And I know my body so much better now. I tell my lover exactly what to do. He satisfies me so much better now! I also find it very empowering to self-pleasure in front of my partner. I'm not needy of his touch, I can give it to myself. Freedom! For me self-pleasure is about pleasure. If it's not pleasurable, something is not right.

So here are the wonderful benefits of self-cultivation.

1. It enhances our sensuality and feminine energy, and thus we become more desirable to our partners.
2. We explore our sexual energy and learn what brings us pleasure so we can share it with our man. He'd be so happy to bring pleasure to his sentient, self-aware woman.
3. We will fill up our love tanks and become magnetic to our partner.
4. We realise that we are our own best lover and stop being needy for any man. That makes us even more desirable in his eyes.
5. We become more attractive to ourselves, and this makes us irresistibly attractive to others.
6. Our experience of sex can become more spiritual.

7. Self-cultivation takes us out of our head and connects us to our body and emotions. It helps us to become more emotionally connected to ourselves and to the people around us.
8. We start to trust ourselves more and open up to our intuition more.
9. It opens the pathway to sexual bliss.
10. Self-cultivation relaxes us and releases stress.

Are you convinced? If not, call me, and I'll think of some more amazingly wonderful reasons for you to practice self-cultivation.

A very important point here: if you feel like you don't really want sex and feel that you have to give it to your man to satisfy his desire, start self-cultivating without having an orgasm at the end. This will increase your sexual energy and will make you want sex more.

If you need more proof on the invaluable and beautiful practice of self-cultivation, listen to this nun's view.

> Masturbation . . . usually does not raise any moral questions at all . . . It is surely the case that many women . . . have found great good in self-pleasuring—perhaps especially in the discovery of their own possibilities for pleasure—something many had not experienced or even known about in their ordinary sexual relations with husbands or lovers.

This is from *Just Love: A Framework for Christian Sexual Ethics* by Sister Margaret A. Farley. Farley has received eleven honorary degrees over her lifetime and is a past president of the Society of Christian Ethics and the Catholic Theological Society of America.

Even the church says pleasure is good for you!

SECRETS OF WEEK 3

1. Fill yourself up with love and joy and give to your man from an overflow.
2. Seven fundamentals to keep us happy:

    a. Movement to feel alive and sensual
    b. Healthy diet to keep us vibrant and nourished
    c. Sleep to feel relaxed and sexy
    d. Spend time with girlfriends to nourish our emotional selves
    e. Time alone and spiritual practice to connect to your feelings, your inner self and the higher energy of the universe
    f. Time spent with nature to purify and energise
    g. Sensual touch and sex to awaken your senses and refuel your bliss tanks

3. Practice self-cultivation to explore your pleasure anatomy and fill yourself up with love.

Practice Week 3

Take your journal out, and write down things that make you feel:

- ❖ Peaceful
- ❖ Joyful
- ❖ Graceful
- ❖ Beautiful
- ❖ Fulfilled
- ❖ Excited
- ❖ Sensual
- ❖ Sexy

Now close your eyes and breathe deeply into your belly, into your hips, into your feet. Scan your body and feel every part of your body. Breathe out any tension you have, imagining your thoughts as bubbles floating in the air. Take a needle and pierce every one of them.

Now ask yourself, "How do you feel?" Welcome all of your feelings. Become curious and see if you can recognise your feelings. What is it that you really feel?

Then ask yourself, "What do you need?"

Listen for the answer and have this inner dialogue:

"I see you need attention, okay. What else do you need? Ah, you need to go for a walk! Okay. What else? You need me stop judging you, okay. What else do you need? I hear you; you need to spend some time by yourself in the morning. I'll see what I can do about it. Thank you so much for sharing. I'll do everything that I can to make you feel better. Let's go for a walk now!"

Write in your journal what you find out about your needs from this inner dialogue.

Homeplay Week 3

1. Connect to Your Feelings

Spend at least five minutes every day this week checking in with yourself and how you feel and dialoguing about your needs. Welcome your feelings without trying to change them, accepting everything that comes.

2. Sensuality Awakening

Sit in the sun somewhere in nature, and touch your hair. Feel the softness and beauty of your hair. Appreciate your own beauty. Breathe into your inner channel, from your yoni into your heart, and breathe out from your heart into your yoni. Feel all your body awakening to pleasure.

3. Fill Up Your Love Tanks

How do you want to feel today? Pick up one or two activities from your list of things you need to do to get into your chosen mood for today and do it.

How are you going to fill your love tanks? I'm excited! Are you? If you are not, maybe that's not what you really want to do.

4. Self-Cultivation Practice

Continue doing your self-cultivation practice and have fun with it.

WEEK 4

Make Him Your Hero

> *Deep inside every man there is a hero or a knight in shining armour. More than anything, he wants to succeed in serving and protecting the woman he loves.*
> *John Gray*

Recognise Your Man as an Expression of the Divine

This chapter is all about your man. As I've already told you, I love men; I love their desire and readiness to make us happy. I admire their loyalty, their sense of honour and reliability. I love their hands, their strong bodies, and their desire to protect us from all the lions around us.

A man is an expression of the divine. Yes, we might want to change some of his humanness, but the essence of him is divine. Do you honour your man? How do you make your man feel? Does he know that he is the one you want to share your life with? Maybe you are upset with him at the moment and you start to wonder if he is really the one for you.

It's so easy for us to emasculate men by criticising them and not trusting their impulses to keep us safe and happy. Yes, sometimes they think they know more about what we need, and it can be annoying. But if we realise that they do it with their best intentions to make us happy, we might reconsider our attitude.

It's a good start to feel grateful for his existence and for his choice of you as his partner. Imagine, from all the women around he chose you! What a miracle.

One of His Top Needs—Significance

Men need to feel significant. He needs to feel that he matters, that he's needed and valuable. If a man doesn't feel significant, he crumbles. He feels defeated and loses the strong masculine qualities that we women admire and need in order to feel safe.

When a man doesn't feel valued, he might withdraw into his own cave, and his woman will feel rejected and lonely. When this happens assume that he is asking for something from you, that he feels unloved and under-valued. However, we should also remember that sometimes men do need time on their own. It's very healthy for them and for the relationship. Never take it personally when a man needs to separate to find his inner centre. It's a huge mistake to try to stop him or punish him for wanting to have his own space for a while. In this instance I am talking about a different kind of withdrawal—a woman-caused withdrawal rather than a healthy need for time and space alone.

> ### A Note on Men
>
> If a man doesn't feel significant in his romantic relationship, he will find a way to fulfil this essential need somewhere else. Maybe by working a lot, maybe by spending most of his spare time with his mates, or maybe by having an affair. The drive to feel significant is so strong a need in a man that he'll find a way to fulfil it.

There are positive and negative ways to fulfil our essential human needs. Sometimes people kill to appear in the press, just to be heard and to feel significant. A child might have a tantrum or break things to get attention and feel that she or he matters. Women often feel significant providing for their children. These tiny bundles of love need us. Men tend to feel significant by working and providing for their family.

It's crucial to make our man feel significant in the relationship; so he knows he's valued and honoured. We need to remember that if we don't make him feel significant, he'll find a way on his own. And it could be a way that we don't particularly like . . . It's up to us to fulfil his need in a way that creates intimacy and harmony in the relationship. Make your man feel significant, and it will draw him to you.

By making him feel significant, we are actually looking after ourselves. We are making sure that the strong man we need is by our side and is able to cherish us and provide what we need.

Does your man feel that he is the most significant person in your life? On a scale of zero to ten, how significant do you think you make him feel? Now, imagine stepping into his body and answering from his point of view.

The secret here is to make him your hero!

A Note on Men

Have you ever wondered why men are so focused on achieving and performing? It's in every man's nature. He desires to be admired as a hero, and he needs our admiration to feel strong and confident. Just as we need caring and adoring attention to feel loving and happy.

Let him know how much he means to you and how happy he makes you. He needs to know that he is your number one. He needs to know that he is successful in making you feel happy. Appreciate every little effort he makes in giving you joy and love, and you will get more of it. Appreciate the effort, not the end result; things sometimes don't work out the way we want them to.

A Note on Men

When a man feels he is a hero, it's a magnificent sight. He is in his power, very fulfilled, and generous to give of himself. Isn't that what we want?

I invite you for the next week to ignore all the problems you might have and only focus on the positive. Notice what he does for you, every little thing. And appreciate him by saying "thank you." Focus on gratitude in your heart for what he does for you.

You might be surprised by how much he does for you—little things that we usually take for granted like opening a door for you, driving you somewhere, making the bed in the morning, cooking dinner, or playing with the kids to give you time to rest.

I assumed that my partner did all these things because he wanted to. What I found out was that if it wasn't for me, he would work or read or surf. It made me realise that I do things just because I know I have to, and no one else will do them. But he does things to make me happy.

Amazing how much effort a man puts into making his woman happy. And how rarely we appreciate it, taking everything for granted, thinking: *Of course he plays with the children, they are his! Of course he does housework, he lives here! Of course he drives when we go on long-distance trips, he is a man! I always do it, of course he has to do it sometimes!*

What changed my attitude was recognising that the intention behind his actions was to make me happy.

Take a moment to pause and notice and appreciate every little thing your partner does for you. Just shift your focus slightly and see all the great things about him, even if there are only a few things. Start somewhere and you will notice how he puts more and more effort into caring for you. Forget about all the negative things you know about him for a week. Focus on all the good qualities he has and things he does for you. Notice how he responds and what happens to your relationship.

A word of caution, however, a woman shouldn't try to manipulate her man by appreciation. Though the result is that her partner will want to give her more love and care, that's not why she appreciates him. She appreciates him because he is her man and she loves him.

A Note on Men

Once a man is her hero, a woman will start to feel like a queen. He'll have the energy to give her the love and care that she needs. And because he feels fulfilled, he'll enjoy cherishing his woman and providing for her.

We have the power! Yes, yes, Beautiful, step into it! Right now, get up, speak your intention to transform your relationship, and make a step forward. With your generous and nurturing love, you can take your relationship to a new level, a new depth of intimacy, and a new pinnacle of pleasure. Isn't it what you desire?

Appreciate Him, Forget Criticising

To keep a lamp burning
we must keep putting oil in it.
Mother Teresa

The best way to make our partner feel significant is to appreciate him for who he is and what he does for us. Especially when we appreciate what he is good at and what he is proud of doing. If we show our appreciation when there are friends or relatives around, our man will feel very special. Don't we all need appreciation? Doesn't it feel good to be appreciated for that cake you put so much effort into or the way you kissed and hugged him? And it feels so wonderful when he admires the new haircut. It's disastrous when he doesn't like it or worse, doesn't even notice it.

We need to forget all about criticising. We should never criticise a man. It doesn't inspire him to change and become a better person. Yes, that's the way we women might change, but not men. It only creates distance and makes him withdraw into his cave. I invite you to upgrade your critic into an appreciator. It is more enjoyable. It brings joy to spread love and appreciation. Are you up for a challenge?

Here is what my beloved man says about appreciation.

Your appreciation fills me up. It feels wonderful. It gives me a sense of security, everything is worthwhile. It makes me want to give back to you.

- ❖ **What makes me feel appreciated:** When I'm listened to, when my advice and opinion is acknowledged and given consideration. When you do something special for me, when you cook for me or spend special time with me. When you acknowledge what I've done well. When you acknowledge my generosity.

- ❖ **How I feel when you don't appreciate me:** I feel angry, resentful, defeated. I feel like there is no point in trying, nothing is good enough. I stop trying, I withdraw and feel insignificant. I don't matter.

- ❖ **How I feel about you when you don't appreciate me:** You look less attractive, and I start to focus on your faults. I tune you out or become more attentive to other things, like my work. Whatever you say I take a negative spin on, and my feeling of not being appreciated aggravates.

It might be hard not to criticise when we feel hurt or not cared for. Our instinctive response is to decrease the power of the one who threatens our well-being (and anything that makes us feel uncomfortable or stressed is read by our primitive brain as threatening). We do this with men by emasculating them. Criticising is a tool we use to emasculate a man, cut him down, and reduce his confidence. Sometimes we emasculate and manipulate by not giving sex, withdrawing our love, or nagging and making our man's life as unpleasant as possible. Then we feel that his power over us is reduced and he is less dangerous.

Men are bigger and stronger, and instinctually we deal with them by emasculating or pleasing. It doesn't matter what our logical mind says. Even if we have several academic degrees and earn lots of money, our primitive brain still says that we are smaller and weaker. And whether we are happy with it or not, our primitive brain gets activated every time we feel threatened.

What's interesting is that we are actually looking for the strongest man, the one who's got more power, more money—the alpha male who can provide and protect. Have you ever thought about why men in leadership roles are so irresistible? My friend was telling me that he was never as popular among women as when he was a ski instructor leading a group through the mountains.

Ironically, once we have found the strongest man, we tend to fight with him to prove that we don't need him and that we are stronger. This is how the pull-push dynamic is created in our intimate relationships. Our primitive brain says we need a strong man by our side to survive, and our logical brain says we are strong and don't really need anyone to take care of us.

There is a constant conflict going on inside us. Sometimes it comes out as an overwhelming urge to tell him his car is dirty when he's all dressed up and is proud to take his woman out; or when we disrespect him by interrupting when he's talking to a group of friends; or when we tell him his suit and shirt don't match when there is no possibility for him to change it; or when we say "Don't you worry about money, I got it all covered, I'll provide for us"; or when we condemn him for not giving his children what they need; or when we don't remind him of our anniversary and then get upset about his forgetfulness and make him feel like a failure. It is not really fair on him, is it? We are ruining both his and our own fundamental happiness when we cut him down to size.

> ### A Note on Men
>
> We don't realise that men love to protect and provide for us not because we are weak and incapable, but because that's what they love doing. They love us, our softness, and our beauty.

I catch myself reacting and getting into fight-or-flight mode. I pause. I breathe. I don't talk. I remind myself of my *goddess truth*:

> I am safe in the universe, all of life loves and protects me. My beloved loves me and wants to make me happy. I love myself. I have the capacity to keep myself safe.

Once I empower myself, I don't have to react and make my partner feel smaller. I don't have to criticise. And this is always a work in progress. Some triggers are way too strong. Sometimes I feel tired and have an urge to let my tiredness out in an argument. I forgive myself. I love myself. I keep on practising.

Listen to Him and Be Curious

Attentive listening makes our partner feel safe and open up to us emotionally. Truly listen, be on his side, and be curious by asking, "Is there anything else you have to say?" Don't try to figure out what you want to say on the topic when he's speaking. Don't agree or disagree. Just be curious and attentive.

A man puts his experience and himself into his opinions. It's an expression of who he is. Like for us our feelings are an expression of who we are. We hate it when men try to change or fix our feelings and tell us we shouldn't feel this way . . . true? Same goes for men; they put themselves into their opinions.

We need to listen and see it as a great way to learn more about our man, who he is, and what he cares about.

A Note on Men

If a woman argues and tries to change a man's opinions, he will feel that she is trying to change him and control him. He will resist and push her away, closing off his heart and emotionally removing himself from the relationship.

Once a woman listens without thinking of how she will reply and how it applies to her, being fully on his side, a man will open up more and more, and she'll experience deeper intimacy. That's how the friendship starts and trust develops.

Melissa is married to Jack; they've been married for almost fifteen years. She came to me for counselling when she started to feel that she couldn't take things the way they were with Jack anymore. Melissa blamed her husband for withdrawing and not wanting to talk to her. It made her feel rejected and lonely. She said he used to be open, and she enjoyed their conversations very much, but now he was just coming home and watching TV or reading. When she tried to talk to him, he seemed disinterested and sometimes even disapproved when she interrupted him. So Melissa dealt with his rejection by blaming Jack and arguing with him—in this way she at least got some of his attention.

The latest argument was apparently about going out to a restaurant at night. Melissa was cooking every night and she suggested they go out to have a break and spend some romantic time together. Jack never liked going out and he resisted, saying that he preferred home-cooked food.

Melissa got irritated. She started arguing and telling her husband how much fun it was to go out, that he never took her to restaurants, that he didn't care about her and that she was bored with him always reading his newspapers. And on and on it went, until the point that Jack got up and went into the garage to check on his fishing gear. Melissa got very upset and started crying. She felt even lonelier as there was no one to comfort her. She wondered where the Jack she knew fifteen years ago had gone. She pondered the fact that maybe it was time to move on and find someone who would love her and talk to her. Melissa said this kind of argument was happening in their relationship all the time.

Together we uncovered her unconscious belief that she was unworthy of love. This belief was deep-rooted in her childhood when her parents separated. She felt it meant that her father left because there was something wrong with Melissa, and she was unworthy of his love. Melissa was able to uncover her inner *goddess truth*.

> I'm love. I deserve to be loved. I share my love with my beloved because I have an infinite amount of it.

After that she was able to listen to Jack and his opinions without reacting to them. She could open up to him and listen to why certain things were important to him and to what influenced his opinions. To her surprise Jack started to talk to Melissa and share what was going on for him. And he became curious about what was happening in Melissa's life, how she was feeling, and how he could support her.

Now, Melissa says that Jack is her best friend and she would never think of leaving him. He is all that she wants and needs.

How Well Do You Know Your Man?

Think of your man.

- ❖ Do you know what your man values in life?
- ❖ What drives him in life?
- ❖ What's important to him?
- ❖ Does he have any goals?
- ❖ Is he trying to achieve something?

Ask him. Let him talk. It can take him a while to get started. Don't offer your view or suggestions after his first sentence. Wait and listen. I know it can be very hard; I count up to ten to make it easier for me not to interrupt.

What we often do is ask a question, and then when a man doesn't reply straight away, we suggest an answer or give him a multiple-choice option. We don't know that men take our questions seriously and want to think before replying. Our interruption tactic disturbs his thought process, frustrates him, and makes him feel that his answer is not important. He starts to wonder, *Why did she ask me in the first place if she's not interested in hearing what I have to say?* And then we wonder why is he not talking to us?

SECRETS OF WEEK 4

1. A man is an expression of the divine.
2. Men need to feel significant. Make him your Hero!
3. When a man doesn't feel valued he withdraws.
4. When a man feels like a hero, he is capable of giving his woman what she needs.
5. Be grateful for every single thing your man does for you so he feels valued and appreciated.
6. Forget about criticising your man. It won't change his behaviour but will push him away.
7. Listen attentively to your partner, and he will open up to you.

Practice Week 4

Tune in to Your Man's Inner World

Find some quiet time, close your eyes, and breathe deeply into your belly, feeling all of your body and relaxing any tension you might have in your body.

Then imagine stepping into your partner's body and feel as if you are him, talk as if you are him. Answer as if you are him the following questions:

- ❖ What do you feel about her?
- ❖ Do you feel loved by her?
- ❖ What do you want from her?
- ❖ Do you have any fears in regards to her?

Talking as if you are your partner will help you to feel him from the inside and get into his energy. You will gain a heartfelt understanding of your partner and open up to his feelings and his inner world.

Then it might be good to share what you find out, and ask him the same questions. It could be fun to compare the answers, but do it without any judgements and certainly without telling him that you know better what he really thinks and feels.

Homeplay Week 4

1. Awakening Your Sensuality Practice

Go for a walk in nature and pay attention to all the smells to wake your senses up. Smell the flowers, wind, sand, and your hands. Become your nose and see the picture of the world through your nose.

2. Gratitude Practice

Every evening write three things in your journal that you are grateful for about your partner.

3. Pause, Notice, and Appreciate

When you are with your man, pause and notice something to appreciate him for. Speak your appreciation. Make it a habit to appreciate him at least twice every day. Be generous. For a more profound effect, appreciate him in front of his friends or relatives for something that he loves doing and is proud of.

WEEK 5

Become a Magnetic Sensual Goddess

There is nothing that so arouses, supports and sustains the normal sex-passion in a man as for a strongly-sexed woman to fill her aura toward him with a strong, steady, self-controlled appeal—tender, loving, admiring, yet deliciously sensuous and aesthetically voluptuous; pure, yet deep, warm, alluring.
J William Lloyd

Understanding Masculine and Feminine Energies

Why are we attracted to each other? What is it about? Sometimes I feel this attraction as a current of electricity that almost lifts my hair. It can be so strong, our bodies drawn to each other with such intensity, utterly magnetised to each other. What is this attraction? Why is it so strong with some men and nonexistent with others? I believe a large part of it is about our opposite polarities. The more polarized our magnets are, the stronger the attraction. Do you want a strong man by your side? A man who is stable, reliable, and able to love you through all your emotional states? If yes, you need to relax more into your soft feminine side to awaken his strong masculine side.

All of us have both masculine and feminine energy. Masculine energy is direct, focused, penetrating, solid, purpose-driven, and structured. It's based on values and thrives on achieving set goals. At times in our lives, we all need masculine energy to achieve our goals, complete projects, and cut through the lies and damaging emotional states.

Feminine energy is fluid, soft, in the moment, changeable, intuitive, love-driven, and nurturing. It's based on emotional states and thrives on relating to others. Men and women need to have access to the feminine energy to create more love, care for others, and build harmonious relationships.

As women it is healthy and fulfilling for us to spend more time in our feminine energy, especially when we are relating to our romantic partner. For men it is healthy and fulfilling to be more often in his masculine energy, especially when he is relating to his beloved woman. That said, it can be very exciting and rewarding to sometimes reverse the energies and explore the other side of ourselves and our partners. This can feel as if you have a relationship with two different people, and then your love life will never be boring.

For the feminine side to uncover herself in her full beauty, she needs to feel safe and supported by the masculine side. To avoid the dependency on our partners, it's a great idea to develop our own inner masculine side so that our feminine side can flourish. A woman with a developed inner masculine aspect has the capacity to dive into her deep femininity when she chooses to, becoming fluid, soft, and magnetic. Such a woman will arouse strong masculinity in her partner. She will be attracted to men with mature masculine qualities and will feel cherished by her man.

Some of us have an immature masculine side, which manifests in qualities such as being competitive, having a controlling attitude, not considering the feelings of others, and focusing on achievements at the expense of our own personal well-being and harmonious relationships. In addition an undeveloped masculine side results in the inability to shift between feminine and masculine energies for the purpose of balance and relatedness. As a result a woman with immature masculine qualities tends to spend more time functioning in her masculine mode. A man of such a woman is likely to function more in his feminine energy and stop developing his masculine qualities. If she is looking for a partner, she will probably attract a softer, indecisive, and emotional man who is immature in his masculine side.

This kind of a relationship is usually out of balance and keeps both partners dissatisfied on a deeper level. She wants her partner to give her stability and provide a space where she feels safe to surrender, flow, and express her emotions. This is the deepest yearning of the feminine. However, she feels like a driving force in such a relationship. This causes her man to feel unworthy and weak, overwhelmed by her emotions and dominating attitude.

The most attractive man for me is the one who is powerful, provides safety, and lives a purposeful life. Equally, he is capable of depth of emotions and free expression of his feelings, and he can recognise and follow his own intuition. This man successfully integrates both the mature masculine and mature feminine. He is not afraid to cut through lies and destructive emotional patterns as well as cry when he feels like it. I'm grateful to have found such a man in my beloved.

Create Sexual Polarity

In truth, we can go to the moon and retain its magic for a lifetime. We can breathe in its spirit and never exhale. We can own the powers of romantic enchantment and experience all of life as a glistening adventure.
Marianne Williamson

To sustain passion in a long-term relationship we need to intensify sexual polarity. We do this through playing with our masculine and feminine energies. A woman usually needs to drop more into her feminine, becoming a magnetic goddess so her man rises in his masculine and their magnets get activated.

The masculine aspect is about directionality while the feminine aspect is about receptivity.

> ### A Note on Men
>
> Men thrive on freedom. It is their highest value.

For women the highest value is love. To create sexual polarity between a man and a woman, the woman needs to become an invitation for love, an expression of her desire for deep love. She needs to open up as a flower. Quite often we are afraid to show the depth of our yearning for love.

Showing our depth can be extremely vulnerable. And it's a very powerful act. This is what creates magnetic attraction between lovers. Don't be afraid to show your yearning for love; this is your real authentic power. Imagine yourself with your man. What do you desire from him? Do you dream to be taken by his love and strength? Do you desire to surrender to love? Invite this by showing your desire for love and becoming a Magnetic Goddess Woman.

Imagine you went to a movie and then decided to go for a walk with your man. The street lights went off. Pitch black. Some unrecognisable noises are coming from the trees on your right. Your man starts to hide behind your back and whinge, "I'm scared! I'm scared! Save me! Let's run away!"

How does this feel? Are you feeling sexually attracted to this kind of a man?

Now imagine you went for holidays to Colorado and rented a nice red BMW, and your man is driving you to the hotel. He enjoys the drive, delights in your company, and is proud of being able to make you happy. You decide that he missed the correct turn and start telling him how to get to your hotel. His happiness instantly evaporates. He starts to feel the same way you would feel if he hid behind your back. He feels distrusted and controlled. His desire to make you happy extinguishes, and he wonders why on earth he put so much effort into this adventure if nothing is good enough for you. He's definitely not sexually attracted to you anymore, just as you wouldn't be attracted to him if he started to hide behind your back when he got scared. And this is the case every time we try to give directions to our man and control or manipulate his behaviour. We depolarise our relationships, and the passion dies out.

Can you think of the ways you control or manipulate your man? Take your journal out and write it down. This will help you become aware of the ways you might sabotage your relationship.

Who is the Magnetic Goddess Woman?

Woman is by birth a Queen of Love.
J William Lloyd

Who is this Magnetic Goddess Woman?

She is soft, receptive, and open to receive her man and his love. Yes, she knows she is powerful and uses her power wisely, without overpowering, instead, attracting and melting. She is deeply connected to herself, has clear boundaries, knows what she wants, and accepts all of her feelings. This allows her to be open and accept her man totally—exactly as he is. And of course she is so sensual, so confident in her own beauty, and absolutely loves sex. She loves sensual pleasure, loves her own body, and is delighted to explore sexual pleasure with her man.

Do you recognise her? She is you!

Perhaps, there are moments when you forget this truth. That's when you begin to feel dissatisfied and that there is something missing from your life. The simple reality is you are missing her—you are missing the goddess part of yourself.

Connect to Your Authenticity

Just remain alive and spontaneous and full of feeling. Wherever your sunflower says the sun is, it is there. Allow the feeling that way. And never listen to any other consideration. This is courage . . . and this is authenticity. Authenticity is one of the greatest values in life. Nothing can be compared to it.
Osho

Our lives can be quite stressful juggling between work, kids, social commitments, and our intimate life. We have to be goal-oriented and active in this society that values achievement. We focus on doing and forget all about simply being. To function effectively in the world, we disconnect from our feelings.

Our men also spend the whole day working and the last thing they want is to come home and meet another high-achieving doer.

> ### A Note on Men
>
> Men are more turned on by seeing a woman connected to her emotions and inner world. A woman full of mystery.

We don't have to be anyone different or impress our partners with our consummate performances. All we need is to be authentic with our feelings. To have synergy between our actions and our feelings. When we are intimately connected to ourselves, that's erotic.

For me it's an extremely painful experience when I can't understand what the person I love is feeling. When people are not honest about what's really going on for them, I feel lonely and disconnected.

People try to be nice and sometimes put on masks. But who is home? Who is really there? Who am I talking to? Please, show yourself to me!

Coming Home Practice

Here is a practice that can dramatically change your relationship. Before meeting your beloved in the evening, after a day at work, spend some time by yourself. Do something for yourself that relaxes you and connects you to your inner world. Maybe it's a walk on the beach feeling sand under your feet or listening to your favourite dreamy music or maybe buying a flower for yourself.

Then inquire: How am I feeling? What's happening inside me? Pause. Breathe. Feel. Drop deeper into yourself. What can you connect to now that is even deeper? And what's deeper?

Maybe there is anger and resentment. The amazing gift you can give to your man is to release all of your pent up emotions before coming home. Do you need a pillow to scream into? Or call a girlfriend and tell her about how bad your boss is, how life is unfair and your man doesn't give you what you need. Our girlfriends have a remarkable capacity to listen. Men don't. It's a torture to men to listen to our complaints when they can't do anything about them. Men love to solve our problems for us. They resent being our rubbish bins.

Become aware of your emotional state. Allow the feelings to be. Release any unwanted emotions. Shift your state to one of acceptance of how things are and deep connection to yourself. Now you are ready to meet your beloved. Once you connect to yourself, you are able to connect to your man.

Embody the Magnetic Goddess

Perhaps you like the concept of becoming an irresistibly attractive goddess for your man, but it's hard for you to feel that yummy juicy you inside. I assure you, it's there—deep inside you waiting to be uncovered. That's why I'm writing this book and doing my work. I think it's a fabulous idea to repopulate our earth with sensual goddesses and have all the pleasure we desire. I know there is a switch in every woman that once turned on makes us sparkle, and flowers start to come out of every part of our bodies.

> My client Carol read a lot about feminine energy, changed the way she acted with men, and tried her best to *behave* in a feminine way. It's wonderful how much work she did and how many things she realised about herself. But just by reading and controlling her behaviour, she didn't change her essence. Her dominant energy was still quite controlling and overpowering. She continued to have problems with trying to be the man in her relationship. She had to take care of her partner. But in truth her heart craved to be deeply loved by a strong masculine man. She wanted to be a woman, to be cherished and adored, to trust her man, and to open up fully to him.
>
> She was desperate and didn't know what else she could do to create a balanced, fulfilling relationship. I supported her in discovering her feminine essence through working with her full body, not just her head. She experienced different energies inside her body and discovered her inner sensual woman, sometimes wild, sometimes soft, but always

irresistibly attractive. She stopped controlling her behaviour and relaxed into *simply being*. She was delighted that she could finally relax and was relieved that being a woman was so much easier than controlling the behaviour and trying to act as a woman. After working with me, she attracted quite a different man—one who is strong and provides safety for Carol's feminine side to flourish.

The homeplays are designed to support you in discovering your own switch. I encourage you to engage in the practices to experience transformation rather than just receive information.

Stay Open and Receptive

For one human being to love another human being: that is perhaps the most difficult task that has been entrusted to us, the ultimate task, the final test and proof, the work for which all other work is mere preparation. Loving does not at first mean merging, surrendering, and uniting with another person—it is a high inducement for the individual to ripen, to become something in himself, to become world, to become world in himself for the sake of another; it is a great, demanding claim on him, something that chooses him and calls him to vast distances.
Rainer Maria Rilke

Receptivity and openness are essential qualities of the goddess. Look at the way our bodies are shaped. Our yonis are made to receive lingam (Tantra word for the much-revered penis, meaning "wand of light"). A man can only come close to a woman if she is open and receptive. Only then can deep intimacy be created. So learning how to stay open is an essential part of a magnetic goddess training.

How do we stay open even when the conflict arises? Let's say you did all the "right things," went for a walk, and spent time with your girlfriend, and now you feel so open and loving, ready for hugs and kisses. But, surprise, he's not. You can see that he's definitely upset by something, and you suspect it's something that happened last night between the two of you. What do you do? Our tendency is to become upset with him, feel rejected, and retreat into the dark night of the soul. Or maybe in the beginning we try to push through our man's closed emotional state, and then when he feels invaded and completely puts his shutters down, we feel rejected and again go deep into darkness.

I noticed doing this myself so many times! What does happen in reality? Why is it so hard to stay connected and intimate with each other, especially when one of us is upset? Of course when I'm happy and my beloved feels balanced and in love with life, we feel deeply connected and loving to each other. But once one of us loses our balance, it all goes to hell. He is hurt by something—I try to get through, get hurt, and feel rejected, and so I shut down. Where did the intimacy go?

What happens is that we expect our partner to behave in a certain way, say give us presents on our birthday or gaze at us with love and be happy to see us. When our partner doesn't do what we expect, we interpret his actions to fit into our world view. "He came home stressed and didn't hug me, didn't even looked at me"; my interpretation could be, "He doesn't care about me, he doesn't love me." Once I believe that, I go into a "hurt-little-girl" mode and pull away from him. It's like telling him, "You hurt me and now I'm going to hurt you." Or in your case it could be that he forgot your anniversary, or didn't take the rubbish out, or came home late, or left his socks on the floor.

Reflect on what it is that triggers you and takes you out of your powerful woman state into your "hurt-little-girl" state. Do you remember the last thing that happened? Close your eyes, breathe, and feel what was happening inside of you. How did you feel and how did you respond to his "hurtful" actions?

My invitation is that you pause when you feel irritated or angry. Breathe deeply into your belly. Feel why it is that you are upset. What is beneath your anger or irritation? What is the interpretation you gave to his actions?

Then remember your *goddess truth* from week two, re-affirm it to yourself, and stay open to your man. Go back to your goddess mode. Stay loving. The skill of switching from a little-girl mode into the goddess mode requires practice. But trust me, once you develop the skill, your life and your relationship will change dramatically. You will become the one steering your life and creating your perfect passionate relationship. The whole world will be at your gorgeous feet!

My client Rebecca shared her experience of coming back home after one of my Passionate Love Adventure workshops.

> I was feeling so good and when he got angry, I still stayed open and loving. I didn't shut myself down. I didn't push to find out what was happening for him. I caught myself getting hurt and jumping into my little-girl mode, but I breathed, re-affirmed my *goddess truth* and stayed calm and loving. That somehow made him feel angrier, he couldn't figure out what was happening. And I still stayed in my goddess mode.

> A miracle happened!
>
> He told me that he felt a change in me and was afraid of losing me. And that he never felt sure if I really loved him, and that made him angry. We talked and talked and talked. Never have I ever felt closer to him. What used to happen before, he would get angry, I would feel hurt and withdraw. Only now I understand that every time, I was losing the opportunity to get closer to him and create more love and understanding in our relationship.

Samantha is married with two children and on the surface seemed to have a smooth relationship with her husband of ten years. This is what she said after attending one of my workshops.

> Before, I thought that when he asked me to clarify my opinions, he was being sceptical, questioning me, and I withdrew, protected myself, and shut down the communication. Now, I just listen and stay open to him, curious. When he sees me being that open, he opens up to me. We started to talk about things, discussing things that we never talked about before. Before, during sex I sometimes didn't feel good, but I would keep silent and let him continue. Now, I always say how I feel. We discuss things, and this has allowed us to explore a lot of new stuff, like sensual massage, breathing exercises together, and even dressing up and getting into all sorts of exciting role playing. This has brought so much spice to our sex life! But it all started with me being open and loving towards him no matter what happens—not going back into my wounded little girl, and staying in my *goddess truth*.

The most important thing for us to do here is to stop taking what our partners say and do personally. Most of the time it's about them, not us. For example, with my ex-partner I used to think that he was bored because I was boring, because I didn't excite him, because he didn't love me, and somehow I wasn't enough to keep him excited about life. So I would withdraw and get angry and sad. After we broke up, I realised that was his way of life. He was bored with life, and it had nothing to do with me. And by shutting down and taking my love away from him, I was making things worse. He felt lonely, I felt hurt, and we just couldn't connect; there was no place for love and intimacy. If I had shared with him how I felt, that his being bored made me feel unwanted, then there would have been a possibility of opening up and becoming intimate. But I was so hurt and just didn't want to admit I was hurt. I spent all of my energy on hiding my hurt feelings and pretending that everything was okay.

A Note on Men

When a man is angry or shutdown, he is actually asking for something from his woman. He feels hurt and that's how he expresses his needs. The most damaging thing a woman can do here is shut down and stop communicating. He is hurting and asking for her love and support. If she doesn't take things personally, stay open and loving, he'll have space to open up and connect with her on a much deeper level. He'll trust her more because he'll know that she accepts his "negative" emotions and cares about his needs. All of us have a tiny, sweet, hurt child inside, and we are all in this together.

If you are unsure how to act, ask "What would love do?" This will be the only true answer.

Secrets of Week 5

1. We all need a balance of mature masculine and mature feminine qualities to be whole and function harmoniously in our relationships.
2. Stay open to him and loving no matter what.
3. Remember your *goddess truth*.

4. Switch back from your "hurt-little-girl" mode into your goddess mode when things are not how you expect them to be.
5. Don't take what he does or says personally.
6. Challenge the assumptions you make about his actions—is this really true? Is it true that he doesn't care about me when he does this? Is it true that he doesn't love me when he does that?

Practice Week 5

Choose a Sexy Name

Think of a forbidden name for yourself, one that shows the side that sexually provokes your partner and teases him. A name that describes your passionate, naughty sexy woman—a woman who is open to take on pleasure and new experiences. Let's unleash your sexy, sensual goddess who brings passion and excitement! It could be something like Babe, Sexy Goddess, Juicy Lucy or Sweet Kitten. The name I like now is Cleopatra. I can feel the sensual magnetic power arising in me just as I write this. Oh where is my beloved? Come home soon!

How do you feel when you are called this name? What is arising in you? Let him know your sexy name that brings out your full passion. Enjoy the ride!

Homeplay Week 5

1. Connect to Your Breasts

Connect to your breasts, touch them and send them love. Your breasts nurture you the same way they are capable of nurturing a baby. Breasts play a very important part in our sexuality and feminine power. Repeat this practice every morning to drop into your femininity. I also like walking around the house topless when it's warm. It makes me look at my breasts all the time and appreciate their beauty. I must tell you, my partner very much enjoys this practice as well.

A note—I can't remember seeing breasts that are not beautiful. If need be, I challenge you to review your perception of your breasts. They are beautiful! It's unavoidable.

2. Engage the Coming Home Practice

Refer to the Coming Home Practice above and practise it every day this week before meeting your man.

WEEK 6

The Way to Delicious Sex

Let your making love be more like a happening than like a making.... How can you make love? It is not something like doing: it is not an action. It is a state. You can be in it but you cannot make it. You can move in it but you cannot do it. You can be loving but you cannot manipulate it....

When you make love, be possessed. Move slowly, touch each other's bodies, play with each other's bodies. The body is like a musical instrument. Don't be in a hurry. Let things grow. If you move slowly, suddenly both your energies will rise together, as if something has possessed you. It will happen instantly and simultaneously together. Then only Tantra is possible. Move now into love....

Osho

What is Sex for You?

. . . we can work toward promoting pleasure and encouraging affectionate interpersonal relationships as a means of combating aggression. We should give priority to body pleasure in the context of meaningful human relationships. [. . .] Affectionately shared physical pleasure tends to stabilise a relationship and eliminate the search.
James Prescott

Okay, let's talk about sex! The most taboo, provocative, and exciting subject.

What happened to me recently? Well, I wanted to give an ad in a local publication to promote my business. When I spoke with them on the phone, I told them I was a relationship coach, and the lady said they would be happy to advertise for me. Once I sent them my ad, which had the word "sex" in it, they said, "We have very strict guidelines as to what advertising we can accept, and we don't feel that yours would be suitable for the publication."

I wonder—how is it possible to talk about intimate relationships without mentioning sex?

So let's talk about sex, that vital and mysterious part of our intimate relationships. I believe that most relationships break down because of sexual tension and dissatisfaction. Though the reasons we give can be quite different.

Do you remember the passion you had in the beginning with your man? Close your eyes and remember what was special about it. Remember your feelings and the sensations in your body.

Do you have intense moments of intimacy with your partner now, when you cry out of joy and love? Do you sometimes feel so open to him in your love that your heart melts?

Or maybe sex feels like just another boring thing to do, a routine, something you need to do for your partner to keep the family together.

It makes me so sad that some women don't enjoy sex and regard it as a burden.

How do you feel about sex? What does it mean to you? Is it something you love and put your full passion into, or is it something that you are not interested in, you don't want to talk about, and you let your man enjoy without your full participation? Or maybe it's something that you feel ashamed of and unsure about?

What is sex for you?

The Importance of Pleasure

James W. Prescott, an American developmental psychologist, undertook research focused on the origins of violence. He studied different cultures and made a correlation between crime rate and openness to sexuality. Interestingly enough, though I believe it is very logical, he found that the more open the culture is to sexuality, the less violence there is. According to his work "Body Pleasure and the Origins of Violence," the most violent societies were those that suppressed sexuality.

> In short, violence may stem from deprivation of somatosensory pleasure either in infancy or in adolescence . . . Physically affectionate human societies are highly unlikely to be physically violent. Accordingly, when physical affection and pleasure during adolescence as well as infancy are related to measures of violence, we find direct evidence of a significant relationship between the punishment of

> premarital sex behaviours and various measures of crime and violence . . . .
>
> Premarital sexual freedom for young people can help reduce violence in a society, and the physical pleasure that youth obtains from sex can offset a lack of physical affection during infancy. Other research also indicates that societies which punish premarital sex are likely to engage in wife purchasing, to worship a high god in human morality, and to practice slavery.
>
> These findings overwhelmingly support the thesis that deprivation of body pleasure throughout life . . . are very closely related to the amount of warfare and interpersonal violence . . . .
>
> It is clear that the world has only limited time to change its custom of resolving conflicts violently. It is uncertain whether we have the time to undo the damage done by countless previous generations, nor do we know how many future generations it will take to transform our psychobiology of violence into one of peace.

Think about Iraq. The violence that still happens there. And the way they generally treat women. From the New York Times, Saturday, October 13, 2012:

> Since the bloodshed peaked in 2006, order was gradually restored, though violence remained high by any but wartime standards. The continuing violence has hampered reconstruction efforts and despite sitting on some of the world's largest oil reserves, Iraq is only the world's 11th largest producer of oil. Corruption and oil smuggling, as well as long-term

economic problems, have also hindered the country's development and millions lack clean drinking water and are reliant on food aid.

In her book *Honour & Shame: Women In Modern Iraq*, Sana al-Khayyat talks about the status of modern women in Iraq. She talks frankly about sex and marriage, physical and mental violence, the fear of scandal, and their indoctrination into the ideology of honour and shame in Iraq. Iraq, as al-Khayyat tells us, is a patriarchal society that suppresses female sexuality. If a woman is immodest or brings shame on her family by her sexual conduct, she brings shame and dishonour on all kin. Husbands assume if they show affection it might "spoil" their wives, who would then take advantage of them and become demanding. Men don't wish to initiate their wives into sexual fulfilment, because they believe it will make them promiscuous.

This supports James W. Prescott's view that there is a direct correlation between violence and sexual suppression.

Do you understand how important your search for increased pleasure is? You are not exploring and freeing your sexuality just for your own pleasure, you are helping to create love and world peace. Isn't it something to be excited about and take very seriously? I hope you are with me and are devoted to experiencing blissful lovemaking with your partner.

Take a stand for yourself now and say it out loud.

> Yes, I am devoted to my own pleasure. I do want to experience blissful lovemaking and create more harmony, intimacy and love with my partner. I reclaim my full sexual goddess power to create love and life. I want to join the pleasure revolution and create more love and peace in this world.

Or something to this effect that sounds true to you.

So what is it that we need to do to reclaim our full, sexual, goddess power and enjoy ecstatic lovemaking? Let's explore!

Feel Good About Your Body

Sex lies at the root of life, and we can never learn reverence for life until we learn reverence for sex.
Havelock Ellis

The most important thing in reclaiming our magnetic feminine power is a need to feel comfortable and confident in our own skin. We need to love our body and be happy to share its delights with our lover. How can we fully enjoy someone touching us and looking at us if we think that the body we were gifted for this life is in some way defective and not good enough?

Is there anything you can do to start loving and appreciating your body more?

The body is a living organism that requires our tender care to show its full potential. I like to think of my body as a gorgeous child. If I condemn my body, it shuts down and doesn't perform at its best; it loses its shape and strength, just as a child would. But if I encourage it, care for it, and love it, it opens all of its miracles and hidden capacities to me; it becomes vibrantly alive and full of pleasure.

Body Appreciation Practice

I invite you to make a list of all the good things your body does for you, so you start appreciating it more.

What do your legs do for you? Perhaps they take you for a walk, move you around to the places you want to be, dance, run, ski, and enable many other activities that bring joy. What are you grateful to your legs for? Write down all the wonderful things your legs do for you and send them gratitude and love. Look at them and see their beauty.

What do you like about your hands? What do they do for you? Can they touch gently and lovingly? Do they cook yummy food for you or drive the car? Write down all the wonderful things your hands do for you and send them gratitude and love. Look at them and see their beauty.

The belly could be a more difficult part for a woman to love. However, it does so much for us. It gives us the opportunity to give birth to our beautiful children. What a miracle! And we rarely appreciate our bellies for their gift of creation. It gives us nourishment and allows us to live in our human form. At one point in our lives, we all were snuggled very warmly in the belly of our mum. Put your hands on your belly. Think of everything it does for you. Send your gratitude and love to this beautiful, soft part of your body.

Go through other parts of your body, think of good things they do for you, and send them love and gratitude.

Become Friends with Your Yoni

In contrast, the ancient Tantric and Taoist reverence for women's sexuality in general, and their genitals in particular, is illustrated by a host of lyrical euphemisms such as "Jade Gate" or "Jade Chamber," "Golden Furrow," "Anemone," "Pearl," "Oyster," "Lotus," "Lyre," and "Phoenix."
Rebecca Chalker

Cultivating the love for our yoni is the second step towards blissful sex. It doesn't matter how amazingly beautiful we look, if we don't feel comfortable with our yoni, our sexual organs, we are not able to relax and fully enjoy lovemaking. The gender difference here is very strong.

A Note on Men

Men are proud of their sexual organs and regard them as a representation of their masculinity.

We women, more than often, don't look at our sexual organs, find them repulsive, and want to hide them away even deeper. This makes it rather hard to find sex fulfilling.

Linda E. Savage says in her book *Reclaiming Goddess Sexuality—The Power of Feminine Way*":

> As much as women complain about their hips, buttocks, breasts, or waistlines, the yoni is at the heart of most women's body-image distortions; it is their ultimate disowned body part. How women

really feel about the seat of their sexuality is a much more serious issue of body image that they rarely, if ever, talk about—even in therapy. Yet these feelings are central to desire disorders in women.

Quite often we just use our bodies without acknowledging what they do for us. Without asking if our bodies are happy with what we are doing to them.

Sometimes we are so disconnected from our bodies and sexual organs that we can get into self-rape—having sex when we don't want to, having sex just to please our man, and allowing men to have their way without enjoying the sexual experience. This needs to stop. It's dishonouring. It's self-destructive and relationship-destructive. It's violence aimed at ourselves.

I invite you to repair the connection with your body and your yoni. I invite you to deeply honour your sacred sexual power.

Become Friends with Your Yoni Practice

I know this practice can sound a bit challenging for some of us. However, it's so important to connect to our sacred sexual organs, to listen to what they have to say, and to become friends with them.

Find some quiet time. Make sure your phone is switched off and no one is going to disturb you.

Find a hand-held mirror and get naked. Breathe deeply into your belly, relax your body, and send love and acceptance into your body, embracing yourself with love.

Then lie down and look at your yoni using the hand-held mirror. Look at her, learn about her shape and folds. Say hi to your yoni and ask her how is she feeling about you looking at her in this way.

Ask: How do you feel about me? What do you have to tell me? Do you think I'm taking a good care of you? What do you need from me? Do you like the way we are making love with my man? What do you think about oral sex? How can I make you feel beautiful and sexy?

And listen. Allow the responses to come out of your mouth without thinking about what to say. It's almost like you are lending your voice to your yoni. If this is a bit challenging, relax, breathe deeply, and imagine you are talking to a friend.

Through establishing connection and acknowledging your beautiful yoni, you will become more attuned to her. You will be able to experience more sensations, feel more confident in your beauty, and do only what feels good for you.

Orgasm is Not the Goal

In successful Karezza (controlled non-seminal intercourse) the sex-organs become quiet, satisfied, demagnetised, as perfectly as by the orgasm, while the rest of the body of each partner glows with a wonderful vigour and conscious joy, or else with a deep, sweet, contentment, as after a happy play; tending to irradiate the whole being with romantic love, and always with an after-feeling of health, purity and wellbeing.
J William Lloyd

The next key principle to know is that orgasm is not the goal of lovemaking.

Lovemaking is all about intimacy and connection. I believe that we crave sex so much because it gives us the most intense moments of connection with another human being. There is a possibility of melting, feeling as one, feeling as if we came back home, and feeling we do belong here and we are a part of everything else. I call this experience connected lovemaking.

When there is no anxiety, ejaculation can be postponed for hours—even for days. And there is no need of it. If the love is deep, both parties can invigorate each other. Then ejaculation completely ceases, and for years two lovers can meet with each other without any ejaculation, without any wastage of energy. They can just relax with each other. Their bodies meet and relax; they enter sex and relax. And sooner or later, sex will not be an excitement. It is an excitement right now. Then it is not an excitement, it is a relaxation, a deep let-go.
Osho

My invitation is to have an agreement with your partner that orgasm is not the aim of your lovemaking. What's important is the process and connection between the two of you. As I have a lot of male clients, I know it can be hard to explain this to men as it's a totally new perspective and a new way of thinking. The usual way of lovemaking is building the tension and then releasing the energy, with the biological reasons to procreate life.

Women are now under great pressure to perform by having orgasms, especially during intercourse. There is also a social pressure that says a woman who has an orgasm is more of a woman, a "real" woman.
Shere Hite

However, once we step out of the procreation model and learn that there is much more to experience when we stay connected with each other, the intimacy deepens immeasurably and the whole lovemaking experience gets to a whole new level of bliss and beauty. In connected lovemaking the sexual passion is transmuted into overwhelming love and tenderness for one's partner. It opens our bodies to the experience of all-encompassing love where there is no "I" and "him," where we melt into each other and feel as one organism, one spirit, one soul.

This is what one of my clients said about his experience of connected lovemaking.

> My relationship with my wife is certainly at a more intimate, loving level. We hug more, look into each other's eyes more, touch and caress each other more, and I feel we make love now rather than having sex.

When we focus on orgasm, we disconnect from each other. Our minds become engrossed in achieving the goal, and we stop being present with our own feelings and focus on our partner. I remember the moments when I was so driven to orgasm that I didn't even notice how I was actually feeling and didn't pay much attention to my partner. It all became about me and my sensations. Then I would feel empty and disappointed after the orgasm. I would ask myself: What was that all about? Why was I so frantic and overpowered by my desire? This taught me that mechanical stimulation oriented on achieving orgasm is not something I'm enthusiastic about. I knew there must be a deeper experience of sex, one where the stars start falling from the sky and where I feel as one with my beloved and all of creation.

I remember times when my former partner would focus on his orgasm and forget all about me. His eyes would glaze as if there was no one home, and I knew he didn't keep me in his heart. All he was focused on was the mechanical friction of his lingam in my yoni. He'd tense up and push towards ejaculation. And I would feel abandoned and used. My body was used for his pleasure, and I allowed it. Sad.

Then he'd become lethargic and fall asleep. Where was the beauty and intimacy?

For some women it's hard to orgasm, and it becomes even more important to withstand the focus on it. The more goal oriented and tense a woman is about climaxing, the harder it is to receive pleasure from sex.

Once a woman relaxes and frees her mind from pursuing that goal, she is able to connect to her body and her lover. She becomes aware of all her senses, and her body is likely to open up to pleasure.

Next, I'll talk about curious effects of orgasm on our relationships.

Negative Effects of Orgasm

The more frequently it [orgasmic sex] is employed, the more love dies, romance evaporates, and a mere sexuality, a matter-of-fact relation, or plain dislike, takes the place of the glamour of courtship days.
J William Lloyd

We are focused on orgasms these days. Women went into goal-oriented mode, and all we want from sex is multiple orgasms. And when we don't orgasm, we feel lesser-than, we feel deprived and in some way defective.

However, the reality is, once we focus on orgasm, we lose the connection to our partner and to the present moment. We crave achieving it, and our whole being tenses up in the effort to get to an orgasm.

Ancient traditions like Tantra and Chinese Tao prescribed to their practitioners to preserve their semen while making love so they could achieve higher states of awareness. However, these teachings were focused on male practitioners, and not much was said about the effect of orgasm on women.

According to some research, orgasms reduce our desire and make our partners less appealing. So the more we orgasm, the sooner we might start desiring other partners.

This is what Marnia Robinson says in her book *Cupid's Poisoned Arrow*:

> Sexual satiety (that "I'm done!" feeling) is a mechanism for causing mates to tire of each other. As the honeymoon neurochemistry wears off, the emotionally distancing effects of exhausting sexual desire become more apparent. Neurochemical fluctuations in the reward circuitry occur after orgasm. They can make a mate look less "rewarding," and we may feel that we are falling out of love—at a gut level (habituation).

Robinson goes into great detail about what happens in our brains and why we lose the attraction for our long-term partners. I highly recommend Robinson's book to soak your brain in this new and very potent concept of the negative effects of orgasm.

> ## A Note on Men
>
> In my work with men and my personal experience, I found that male ejaculation does indeed lessen their desire for their partner. After ejaculating men don't find women as attractive as before. They often feel low in energy and tend to start shifting their attention from their woman to work or hobbies. Also—oh ouch!—they start to perceive other women as more attractive. There is simply more mystery and magnetism about the unexplored plains and curves. And women believe sex brings men closer . . . It's an irony and can be very painful.

From my experimenting with orgasmic versus non-orgasmic lovemaking, I discovered that I feel warm and wonderful after I have an orgasm. However, as time passes I start to feel overly attached to my partner and very dependent on him. I describe myself in this state as an energy-sucking jellyfish. It's good if he's got extra time to spend with me and be gentle with me. But if he has to work and is just not in the mood to hold me and console me, I feel abandoned and not wanted. I lose my balance, become emotionally needy and sad, and feel disconnected from the world. I feel no joy and start to question my life choices, thinking that maybe somewhere out there life is much better. Then after a couple of days, I start to see the negative traits in my partner and get frustrated and irritated, again thinking that maybe somewhere out there, with someone else, life would be so much better.

For some time I believed that only men are affected by orgasm with ejaculation, but now I'm convinced that women are affected by orgasms as well.

I'm not saying that everyone has the same experience; I just invite you to become a detective of your own life and find out what your own experience is. Reflect in your journal for two weeks, noting your moods and thoughts, to discover how orgasms affect your emotional state. An approach that works is to have three to four weeks without orgasms, and then allow yourself to achieve orgasm and see how your body and brain chemistry reacts.

According to Marnia Robinson, our gene program is in conflict with our desire for love and a stable, nurturing relationship. Our genes drive us to have as many partners as possible to assure that our offsprings have the best chances of survival. It's the same as the diversification concept familiar to financial investors, which says that you definitely don't want to invest all of your money into just shares, especially shares of just one company. This is imprudent. Portfolio diversification is what they call it in financial terms.

The same logic applies to our genes. What are our genes most concerned with? Yes, survival of the species. Not the long-term loving relationships, which are good for our families and spirit. Consider this: if there was an epidemic, at least one of your kids would have a greater chance of survival if they had a different father and therefore a different genetic makeup and a different immune system. Portfolio diversification! It's only logical.

Our survival system utilises orgasms to drive us away from our partners. After orgasms the brain chemistry changes; we get a kind of "orgasmic" hangover, and it takes about two weeks for our brain chemistry to get back in balance. This affects people in different ways. Some might feel intimate and loving for the first couple of days and then start reacting to the partner negatively. Some people feel flat and unmotivated straight after orgasm and wonder what it was that attracted them to their partner in the first place. As time progresses we start seeing our partner in a different light. It's not that our partner changes, it's our perception of him that changes.

And yet our human spirit and the emotional and spiritual development of our children benefit from long-term stable and loving relationships.

The way out of this is to make love without orgasms and put all the attention on the intimate connection with one's lover. Not many men know this, but orgasm and ejaculation are two different things. With practice men can have orgasms without ejaculation, and their experience becomes much more profound and even spiritual.

> *I have been told that Harry Gaze, the Western lecturer, advocates Karezza* [a method of sexual intercourse where the male partner does not orgasm] *as a means of maintaining eternal youth, and personally I am convinced that nothing else known is so efficient in preserving youth, hope, beauty, romance and the joy of life.*
> J William Lloyd

Luckily, we women don't have to worry about ejaculatory control. All we need to do is relax, stay in the heart, and connect deeply to our partner. Catch yourself when the desire to orgasm takes you away from your partner and present moment. Ask him to pause, then breathe and relax.

It's miraculous what can happen with the relationship when we practice this connected way of lovemaking.

My Experience of Connected Lovemaking

Breathing.
Seeing me in you,
Being here now,
Loving every sigh.
Sister Moon in me.
Meeting you and loving,
Open, flying, crying.
What am I today?
Pulsing in your eyes,
Screaming in my heart.
Who are you today?
Where did we go?
Are we coming back?

I remember how it was before learning this new way of connected lovemaking. I felt used and disconnected from my partner when he was close to an orgasm. His energy would noticeably shift from me and our love and turn into the urge to ejaculate. I wasn't in the picture anymore. And then he would lay exhausted while I was struggling with feelings of sadness and abandonment. I had no idea why. I thought that it was my womanly burden or that I was way too sensitive and expected god-knows-what from an ordinary act of sex. The voice inside was saying, "Grow up! Accept things as they are!" I'm so blessed I haven't.

The experience I have now is completely different. It is a sharing of love. We are together. We are connected. He sees me and I see him. I'm so open to him, to his love, and to his body. My body breathes, moves with the wind of our love, and opens even deeper. Looking into his eyes is scary and exciting. Part of me wants to hide away and is afraid he'll see the very depth of my being. A fear of being hurt arises. And I choose to stay, love my fears, and open even deeper. Love and gratitude envelop me. Now, it doesn't matter where he touches me; my whole body is electrified and full of pleasure. We are together. So much joy! So much love. Nowhere to go, just being in the moment and sinking into the delight of my being—meeting the other being in purity and love.

Our desire to be with each other is stronger and more consistent. Hugging, laughing, and kissing are so appealing.

And then, one day, we slip into orgasm and go through about two weeks of orgasmic hangover with some emotional disturbances and distorted perception of each other.

I start to feel:

> *Oh, no, I don't think he's the one, I don't love him anymore, I think I need to open up and attract someone better. He can't satisfy my deepest desires, I won't be happy with him.*

His mind says:

> *She's not that attractive anymore. That woman I met the other day is more attractive; I think she'll be much better for me. Why is she so critical of me and nothing is ever enough? I don't really feel like spending time with her. I need to work, and I need to spend more time with my friends and do things that I love.*

I found that if I stay in my *goddess truth*—"I'm a blessing to people around me, I'm a powerful beautiful Goddess"—I don't react, and I stay loving to myself. After about two weeks, what a miracle, I love him all over again, and he's looking forward to spending intimate, loving time with me.

How to Introduce Connected Lovemaking to Your Partner

As doctors, the Taoist masters were interested in sexuality as part of a larger concern for the health of the entire body. They practiced Sexual Kung Fu because they discovered that ejaculation drains a man's energy. You have probably also noticed this loss of energy and general feeling of fatigue after ejaculating. Even though you would like to be attentive to your partner's sexual and emotional needs, all your body wants to do is sleep.
Mantak Chia

It's a sensitive subject to talk to your man about changing the way you make love. Even more so to ask him about experimenting with lovemaking without ejaculation.

Here are some tips on how to open your man to a new way of lovemaking. This is not a one-day process and might require a couple of months of your love, acceptance, and appreciation.

First of all acquire some extra knowledge of the subject and talk to your man about what you've learnt.

- ❖ Read some books on the subject such as *Cupid's Poisoned Arrow: from Habit to Harmony in Sexual Relationships* by Marnia Robinson, *Multi-orgasmic Man* by Mantak Chia or *The Karezza Method* by J. William Lloyd (out of print but the full text is available here: www.reuniting.info/download/pdf/TheKarezzaMethodfv.pdf—only thirty pages long).

- ❖ Tell him how much you love him and appreciate him.
- ❖ Stay in your *goddess truth*.
- ❖ Talk to him about what you've read.
- ❖ He might be interested in reading the books himself, if not, don't push it.

Next, create an experience for the two of you with the elements of connected lovemaking.

- ❖ Give him lots of sensual touch without focusing on his genitals; feel love coming out of your fingers. Touch him as if his body is the most precious and beautiful body you've ever touched.
- ❖ During lovemaking stay connected with him, look at him, and touch him all over his body so he starts to feel how it is to spread the energy throughout his body and understands that he can feel much more if he doesn't just focus on his genitals.

Then talk to him about your desire to try connected lovemaking and what it means to you.

- ❖ Tell him you'd love to deepen the intimacy between the two of you and would like to bring more excitement into the relationship because you love him so much and you value the relationship.
- ❖ Stay in your *goddess truth*.
- ❖ Ask him if he'd be open to trying a different way of lovemaking that will greatly increase your pleasure.
- ❖ Tell him that you'd love to try a very slow and sensuous way of lovemaking that will significantly enhance your enjoyment of sex.

- ❖ Whatever he says stay in your *goddess truth*.
- ❖ During lovemaking ask him to pause so you can catch your breath and feel more.
- ❖ Continue giving him lots of sensual touch to awaken his body to more sensations.

The most important factor—don't give up and don't push. Stay in your truth and in what is authentic for you.

This whole process depends on you being patient and loving. If you stay in your *goddess truth* and regularly fill your love tanks, he won't want to resist you. He will want to deepen the intimacy with you and give you exquisite pleasure.

A Note on Men

Men love women who love having sex with them! It boosts their confidence and self-image. He wants you to savour sex with him, so nature is on your side.

Men love adventure and novelty. You only need to figure out how to sell him connected lovemaking as a new adventure that will bring a snowfall of new sensations and experiences into your sex life.

It takes about six weeks of no ejaculation to rewire the brain and about three weeks for the body to start to reabsorb semen. Be patient.

If Your Man Has Sexual Performance Issues

Men's semen is their life force. If they lose it all the time and don't allow this powerful energy to reabsorb into the body, not only do they start seeing their partner as less desirable, but they also might develop an erectile dysfunction, like premature ejaculation or an insufficient erection.

> ### A Note on Men
>
> For men sexual performance issues are a great cause of distress and loss of confidence. Men are very sensitive about their sexual performance and most often have their identity tied up with their genitals and sexuality. If I ask a man where his masculinity resides, most probably he'll point to his genitals.

In contrast women try to forget about their yoni and tend to associate their femininity with their feelings and loving heart.

We need to be very respectful and caring if a man has performance anxiety and treat it with love and acceptance. I know it might be hard to be accepting when we want sex and he doesn't seem to be interested or loses his erection. A woman usually decides, "he doesn't want me anymore," or "I'm not attractive enough" and gets hurt.

However, most of the time it's not her fault. But she can aggravate matters if she reacts and either withdraws from the relationship or blames him for not loving her. Her man will feel devastated because he can't perform and make his woman happy. He will feel judged and will withdraw from a relationship. And, yes, he might start looking for faults in her to justify his lack of desire.

To turn this around, we need to remember our *goddess truth* and respond with love and acceptance. "I'm love. I'm a sexy magnetic woman. I'm a blessing to my beloved." From this space we are able to find the love and acceptance our man needs. If we remain truly convinced of how desirable we are, it will be impossible for us to think that we are "unworthy" and at fault. But if we react from our "hurt-little-girl" space of "I'm not wanted, I don't deserve love, and I'm not enough," then chances are we will drive him away and step into a cold-war realm.

The practice of lovemaking without ejaculation is a very potent tool in overcoming any performance issues in men. And this practice is so enjoyable.

What Does Sex Provide to You and Your Partner?

Denying the body intimacy & sexual release is denying some of the greatest pleasure the body can have. This goes against our biological pleasure principle. We become cut off from our ground, our wholeness, our sense of inner satisfaction and peace.
Anodea Judith

Now to the next step—exploring what sex brings to you and your partner.

How do you want to feel during sex? We don't always want to orgasm. Sometimes we just want a particular feeling, like connection, joy, or a sense of being cared for.

Share with your partner what sex provides for you. What do you want to experience? What do you want to feel?

Next, find out what sex provides for your partner? How does he want to feel?

Schedule a Date at Least Once a Week

Love alters not with his brief hours and weeks,
But bears it out . . . Even to the edge of doom.
If this be error and upon me proved,
I never writ, nor no man ever loved.
William Shakespeare

It doesn't mean that the more time you spend with your man the less passion you have. It doesn't have to be this way, and this is not true. But the closer the two of you become and the more intimacy you enjoy, the less sexual you might start to feel.

The secret here is to have a regular date scheduled in your diary, say once a week. And stick to this date. Don't wait for your hormones to tell you that you need to have sex. It may happen quite rarely for the two of you to have sexual desire at the same time, considering all other commitments, work, and children. Don't you always feel good once the flames get ignited and your body is awakened with passion? Usually, it's the starting that can be a bit of a challenge, just like driving a manual car. Once at full speed, it's a joy to drive. So to make your love life happening and vibrant, just have a date and stick to it. Kindle your desire using the practices in this chapter, and ride the pleasure wave at least once a week.

Create an Inviting Ambience for Lovemaking

Gamble everything for love if you are a true human being.
Rumi

The next step in preparation for delicious lovemaking is to make it a special occasion and create a romantic environment where you can totally relax. Nowhere to go, nothing to do, just being together exploring your sensations and each other's bodies.

First, arrange to have all the time you need. Make sure your kids are looked after and there are no other disturbances.

Then create an erotic ambience. Redecorate your bedroom; make it a sacred space and have something special, say a blanket to cover your bed for your time together. Think of something nice to smell like flowers or essential oils. Light some candles, and put soft, sensual music on.

Do something for yourself to make you feel beautiful, relaxed, and sexy. Maybe have a bath and put on some flowing clothing and sexy underwear.

You are ready! Enjoy.

SECRETS OF WEEK 6

1. Discover what sex means to you and your partner.
2. Realise that you are not exploring your sexuality just for your own pleasure—you are helping to create love and world peace.

3. We need to feel good about our bodies to feel confident and sexy.
4. Cultivate love for your yoni to open up the possibilities for blissful sex.
5. Let the connection with your partner, not orgasm, be the goal of your lovemaking.
6. Orgasm can make our partners less appealing and new partners more desirable. Explore what orgasm does to you.
7. If your partner has a performance anxiety, treat it with love, respect, and acceptance.
8. Discover what sex provides to your partner.
9. Schedule a date at least once a week to keep the passion in your relationship flowing.
10. Create an inviting ambience for lovemaking.

Practice Week 6

1. Explore Your Relationship with Sex

Write down what sex means to you. What happens to you when you say words such as orgasm, clitoris, penis, and ejaculation?

2. Appreciate the Unique Beauty of Your Body

In the morning stand in front of a full-length mirror and spend some time seeing yourself in your feminine beauty. Breathe deeply into your hips; notice your curves and the delicious power of your hips. Find a part that you like on your body. Focus all your attention on that part, forget anything that doesn't survive your scrutiny. Breathe into that part, and expand the sensuality through your body.

3. Become Friends with Your Yoni

Repeat the **Become Friends with Your Yoni** practice two to three times this week, as described in the chapter.

Homeplay Week 6

Set a date and create a romantic ambience. Practice connected lovemaking.

WEEK 7

Ancient, Yet Simple, Tools to Have All the Pleasure You Desire

Sexuality is a sacred ritual of union through the celebration of difference. An expansive movement of the life force, it is the dance that balances, restores, renews, reproduces. It is the production ground of all new life and in that sense—of the future. Sexuality is a life force.
Anodea Judith

Share with Him Your Desires

After exploring your own body you are ready to share openly what you need and what brings you pleasure. Remember, he wants to give you pleasure. But he needs to know how.

Tell him your desires.

If it's not easy for you, know that you are not alone. It took me quite a bit of time and delving into the depths of my psyche before I could openly talk about what gives me pleasure.

But I don't want you to waste your pleasurable time.

So, stand in front of your mirror and reveal everything you want your lover to do to bring you to ecstasy.

And do it again.

And again.

Next time, when you are with your lover, take a deep breath, stay in your *goddess truth*, and share with him what brings you ecstatic pleasure. Your relationship will only benefit.

What could happen if you do share your desires? What could happen if you don't? Which one do you choose?

Movement, Breath, and Sound

The three keys to sexual pleasure are movement, breath, and sound.

These keys help us move the energy in our body and connect us deeper to all of our feelings and sensations.

It's easy for women to switch off and allow the partner to do what he wants. We might dissociate from what's happening and lapse into daydreaming.

> ## A Note on Men
>
> Men told me that sex is frustrating when a woman doesn't participate and is absent from the experience.

If we move our bodies and stay engaged, our experience of lovemaking is more profound. I find that movement opens up and energises my body. It allows me to be fully present to the experience and to not get caught-up in thoughts. Just a gentle flowing movement is all that is required to feel my whole body and deepen my experience.

Sound also intensifies our experiences. Our voice is connected to our sex centre, so using our voice stimulates our yoni and sexual energy. Have you ever made love to someone who was completely silent? Sound connects us to our partner and lets him know what we like and how we feel. It encourages him, and quite often men find our moans electrifying.

Breath gives us life and opens our feelings. It is possible to experience sexual arousal and even orgasm through breathing, rocking the pelvic area, and squeezing pubococcygeus (PC) muscles, the muscles you can voluntary tighten using Kegel exercises (these are the same muscles that we use to stop the flow of urine). If you stop feeling, then pause and breathe.

Freeing Your Voice During Lovemaking Practice

It was not into my ear you whispered, but into my heart. It was not my lips you kissed, but my soul.
Judy Garland

Make a date with your lover, and agree to share, without inhibitions, what both of you feel while making love. The point is to say everything that comes to you without withholding. This practice is about expressing yourself freely, not listening to your partner—an amazingly freeing experience.

Breathing Together and Eye Gazing

One regret
Dear world
I am determined not to have
When I'm lying on my deathbed
Is that I did not love enough
Author unknown, retold by Ocean

Notice, how deeply you are breathing. Do you tend to hold your breath when making love with your partner?

Breath is an essential tool in lovemaking. Only when we are fully breathing do we get back into our bodies and become able to enjoy our yummy sensuality. Breathing takes us deeper and deeper into ourselves and allows us to experience the bliss of physical intimacy.

If you look at babies, they breathe with their whole bodies, and they freely express all of their emotions. That's why children are so full of energy and have that amazing look of wonder on their faces—*What's next? I want to enjoy more of life!*

The older we become, the shallower our breath gets, and we cut off from some of our feelings. If you want to experience more pleasure during lovemaking, breathe deeply into your belly, and allow all of your emotions to rise.

How do you start your lovemaking? Quite often people act habitually and jump straight into sexual stimulation. And it can be sexually arousing, but it's very hard to create a deep connection between lovers who are already going full steam ahead.

It's essential to create a connection before going into sex and to become attuned to each other so that you both feel what the other needs and desires. Then lovemaking becomes a dance, a beautiful and connected dance of love.

The best way to create a connection is by breathing together and eye gazing. You can sit or lie down facing each other and breathe, synchronising your breathing patterns. Look deeply into each other's eyes, and see each other's beauty, power, and vulnerability. Remember, vulnerability is strength. It takes a lot of courage to let others see your vulnerability and softness. Cherish the moments when you are fully open to the other and your soul is flowing out of your eyes.

Eye gazing and breathing together will create trust, openness, and synchronicity between you. When you breathe together, your heart rate and brain waves will synchronise. You will get on the same page and will be able to feel each other better, to understand intuitively what your partner needs.

Pause, Look at Each Other, and Breathe

If you like doing something, do it sweet and slow
My brother Sadiq

Have you ever noticed how too much movement and action takes you away from your feelings? That's exactly how sex becomes mechanical and we require more and more outrageous inventions to become sexually excited.

What if you just paused? There is a lot happening in our bodies and emotions during sex, and to feel all the subtleties of our experience, we need to allow ourselves plenty of time. Otherwise we miss the exquisiteness of tiny movements: the spark in the eye of our beloved and the butterflies in our stomach. We jump on a highway, possessed by speed, not noticing the colours and flowers around us.

Make it a point to pause and feel. Look at each other and breathe. Remember, sex is all about connection, not action.

Looking at each other during lovemaking is a very powerful experience. You can even look at each other during orgasm. This is the moment when both of you are fully open and there are no masks or pretensions. The truth of you comes out. You will see deeply into each other.

It gives me an immense amount of pleasure to see into my partner and to be seen. And, yes, it can be scary sometimes. It feels like there is too much intimacy, and my complete inability to hide takes my breath away. I welcome my fears and choose to open up. There is so much beauty in these fragile moments of vulnerability.

Eye gazing during sex is the most powerful practice for me to connect soul to soul to my lover. It brings profound beauty and love into our lovemaking.

Touching Each Other with Full Presence

Ecstatic lovemaking is all about taking one's time and exploring new ways of being and interacting.

The following practice will take you on a journey of pleasure and sensual awakening. The most essential key for this practice, as is true for any other practice in this book, is to be fully present with yourself and your partner when you are receiving or giving touch.

In our modern busy lives, we are so engrossed in doing and achieving that our senses are often dulled.

- ❖ Do you feel connected to your body?
- ❖ Do you savour your food?
- ❖ Are you fully present when you relate to others?
- ❖ Do you listen attentively and really hear what the other is saying?

We are capable of so much pleasure! Are you ready to fully step into your body and become an ecstatic pleasure goddess?

Touch is one of the greatest ways to step into this experience. Do you know that babies don't survive if they don't get at least *some* touch?

Human beings love to be touched, and for most people an intimate relationship is the only place where the crucial need of touch can be satisfied.

Many of my male clients start crying when I simply put my hand on their head and heart with the intention to nourish. They say, "My wife rarely touches me like that. I so need it. Just a loving warm touch. I miss touch, and I don't understand why we stopped doing it."

- ❖ Do you get enough touch?
- ❖ Do you give a lot of sensual loving touch to your partner?

Conscious Sensual Touch Practice

I invite you to practice conscious and sensual touch with your lover. As you are the one reading this book, I suggest that you give the touch first. Then, after your lover is bathed in love and connected to his body, you can ask him to do the same for you.

You will need several things for this practice.

1. Feathers
2. A soft, silky sheet or a piece of fabric
3. Some fur
4. Your warm, loving hands

Make sure the room is warm, and invite your partner to undress and lie on his tummy. Soft music will help you create a relaxing and romantic atmosphere.

Start feathering over his whole body, and do it very, very slowly. Repeat a minimum five times.

Cover his body with a soft, silky sheet, and move it slowly over his body, pulling it in different directions and sliding across his whole body.

Then touch your lover with the fur—do it slowly and be fully present.

Touch lightly his whole body with your fingertips, slowly and sensually.

Finally, massage his head with your hands, and ask your partner to turn over. Do the same sequence on the other side of his body.

Remember to stay fully present, actively sending love to your beloved. Enjoy touching. Enjoy giving love to your partner, and it will fill you up as well.

The secret is to do everything very slowly. It will allow your partner to experience many more sensations, fully relax into pleasure, and let go.

Now, it's your turn to awaken your senses and enjoy slow sensuous touch!

Explore Taste, Sound, Touch, and Smell Practice

Sometimes, you might want to expand on the touch practice above and include awakening all of your and your lover's senses.

Start with your lover lying down passively with his eyes closed or, even better, covered. Then pick up various musical instruments and bells and play them moving around your lover's body. Then touch all over his body with different materials like fur, silk, your hair, and your fingertips. Remember to go very slowly and be fully present with your touch. Imagine love and warmth flowing out of your hands.

Next, offer various things for him to smell. They should all have a pleasant smell. You can use coffee beans, essential oils, fruits, or flowers.

Last, offer him small bites of aphrodisiac foods like berries, chillies, chocolate, grapes, figs, or bananas. Offer him a variety of tastes such as sour, sweet, salty, and spicy to stimulate the full spectrum of taste.

Then it's your turn.

This practice can sound simple, but it brings remarkable amounts of exquisite pleasure to both the giver and the receiver. It has the power to open all of your senses and take you out of your head and fully into your body. In this state of heightened awareness, the lovemaking can be incredible and take you to a completely new level of ecstasy.

Dressing Up and Role Playing

How do you like getting into different roles and exploring unknown parts of yourself? Usually, in our lives, we act a certain way, have a certain identity, and allow ourselves to just be that known persona. This self-imposed limitation can become quite boring in sexual life.

Human beings have two conflicting needs: certainty (safety) and uncertainty (variety). Love and intimacy require a great amount of safety to flourish. Passion, on the other hand, thrives on variety and uncertainty. The question is, how can we balance these two needs to create deep intimacy and keep the passion alive?

Always acting the same way, touching each other the same way, and even moaning the exact same way is dreadful to any relationship. Life becomes mechanical. We move on autopilot thinking we know all the corners, and there will be nothing unpredictable. It's like driving on the same round for the hundredth time—our consciousness drifts away from the driving, leaving our hands, legs, and eyes to act mechanically.

Is this how we want to make love?

Role playing opens up new possibilities. More importantly, it shows us that what we thought about ourselves is not exactly true. We do have other sides to ourselves that were dormant for years because they were not part of our identity. Role playing allows us to reclaim these forgotten parts and makes us whole. We gain more vibrancy and spice, and we step into our authenticity. It's the difference between two-dimensional and three-dimensional movies. Most of us live two-dimensional lives and wonder why we feel stuck and only half alive.

Explore the fullness of your own being.

A good start is to reverse the roles—you act as a man while your man explores his feminine side. This will allow you to feel what it is like to be in a male body. You won't have to think about what men feel and want. You will have a direct experience of what it is. Just dress appropriately and start pretending. Your body and your being will know how to act because, as I said before, all of us have feminine and masculine qualities.

I was astounded by the level of desire I felt for women when exploring my masculine side. I realised how strong their desire to procreate is. I felt the frustration and pain men have to go through when they have to work hard to get sex or are rejected and shamed for their desire. Women sometimes say that all men want is sex, and we put them down for that. What I felt in my body was a strong biological impulse to create life. How can anyone be shamed for it? Being born in a male body, they didn't have much choice but to have a strong sexual drive. The primal, biological part of every man wants sex and more sex and sex with different partners. It's what they do with it that matters.

Another revelation when exploring my masculine side was how magnetic feminine softness is. The masculine in me was drawn deeply by the receptivity and sensuality of the feminine qualities of my partner. It awoke the noble desire to serve and protect. I embodied this knowledge, and now it's much easier for me to glide into my femininity and magnetise my man into love.

You might want to explore your wild side and dress up as your favourite animal. Or become a goddess and see where it takes you. Choose a role that calls you and play with it. It will spice up your love life and bring you closer to who you are.

Secrets of Week 7

1. Your man wants to make you happy. Let him know how—share your desires with him.
2. Movement, breath, and sound are three essential keys to sexual pleasure.
3. Move your body and stay engaged with your partner to open up to more pleasure.
4. Use your voice during lovemaking to intensify your experience.
5. Breathe deeply to open up your body to more feelings and sensations.
6. Connect to your partner and create synchronicity before jumping into sex, by breathing together and eye gazing.
7. Pause, look at each other, and breathe often during lovemaking to feel all the subtleties of your sensations and create deeper intimacy with your partner.
8. Practise conscious loving touch with your partner as if touching him with your heart. Touch is an essential human need, we can't survive without it.
9. Explore taste, sound, touch, and smell to awaken your abundant sensuality.
10. Get into role playing to discover various hidden parts of yourself and bring more excitement into your lovemaking. Feel in your own body what it is like to be a man, to understand what drives him from inside.

Practice Week 7

Find Your Edge

Write about your fantasies. What is it that you always wanted to explore with your lover? Set yourself free.

What fears come up for you when you write about your fantasies? Step into your *goddess truth* and see if the fears are still overwhelming.

What steps can you take to experience one of your fantasies?

Homeplay Week 7

During the next four weeks, arrange at least one hot date a week with your partner and try the following exercises. Tell him how much you love him and appreciate him. Tell him that your relationship is very important to you and that you want to explore and deepen the intimacy between the two of you. Ask him what he thinks about it and if he has any suggestions. Suggest the following exercises to him.

1. Before Making Love Breathe with Your Partner, Mirroring His Breathing Pattern

Set a date and create ambience for connected lovemaking. Start with connecting to your lover through breathing and eye gazing. This will put you in sync and create an intimate trusting connection between you. Lovemaking can go to a whole new level from this place of being deeply connected with your partner and will open the doors to sexual ecstasy.

2. Relax into Lovemaking and Pause Often to Breathe and Feel

Focus on your deep belly breathing during lovemaking. This will draw your attention to the current moment and relax you. You will slow down and experience all the subtleties of your sensations, expanding your sensuality and sexual pleasure. Deep belly breathing will help you to circulate your sexual energy around your body to allow you to experience full-body blissful pleasure. It would help to ask your man at the start of your lovemaking to support you in what you are trying to do and to pause when you ask him to.

3. Set a Date to Explore One of Your Fantasies with Your Partner

What is it that you always wanted to do but did not dare, for fear of his judgement? Acting out our fantasies has the potential to create more trust and bring novelty into your lovemaking.

4. Explore Role Reversals

Make a date with your partner to explore your masculine and his feminine side. Feel the masculine energy, dress appropriately, and lead your partner as if you were the man. You will have a lot of fun, and also this can be a transformational experience as you will get into his skin, feel what it means to be a man, and understand his concerns and insecurities. He will realise how vulnerable and sensitive it is to be a woman. Then, when you go back into your usual roles, you will be much more sensitive to each other.

When I suggested this practice to one of my clients, his eyes lit up when he considered the possibility of his wife taking a male position and acting dominantly. "How exciting," he said.

Finale

What a journey! Thank you for walking with me along this path. I hope you followed all the steps and played with different practices.

Take some time now to reflect on:

- ❖ What you've learnt
- ❖ How you've changed
- ❖ Where your relationship is now compared to when you started on our journey with this book

Transformation takes commitment and effort. It takes time. Where you are now is a reflection of the level of your commitment. If you feel you haven't moved on much, review your intention and increase your commitment to creating the life and relationship that you desire.

No matter where you feel you are on your journey, celebrate yourself. Step into your *goddess truth* and realise that you are beautiful, powerful, and needed on this earth.

I truly believe you can have the deeply fulfilling relationship you desire. You were born to experience the ecstasy of love.

You wouldn't think of fixing your own car unless you were a mechanic, right? Why do we resist asking for help when we have relationship issues? Why do we treat relationship problems as our personal failure, as if we have all been taught at school how to create harmonious loving relationships?

Here is what my client William, who works as a mechanic, says.

> Before I went to coaching from Tarisha, my relationship of nearly thirty years was at an all-time low (and had been for while). We rarely were intimate with each other, and sex was almost nonexistent.
>
> I had read loads of books on the topic and done couple and individual counselling in the past, with little effect. My wife would say to me about our love life and relationship, "You just don't get it do you?" And she was right! But she didn't seem to want to help out by telling me "what I didn't get."
>
> From my perspective I wasn't getting the love and connection I desired from our relationship, and my being a nice, loving man, helping out at home, or doing things with our children had no or minimal effect on how things were.
>
> In my work as a mechanic, when a customer brings their vehicle in, I often know what is wrong within a few minutes of checking the vehicle over.
>
> Tarisha was like that about my relationship with my wife. After a few sessions with Tarisha, it had changed markedly, and my wife can now be heard saying to me, "Now you get it!" Or "Now you're

talking my language!" We are intimate with each other now. I feel wanted and significant.

The key for me, with Tarisha's guidance, was understanding what was going on inside me and learning about myself. Plus, Tarisha's unique intuition and relationship knowledge guided me to learn the language that had been there all along, that my wife had been "trying to tell me."

We all need to create a support structure around us, to gracefully move forward in any part of our lives. Engage your girlfriends to support you in transforming your relationship and talk through any difficulties you might be having.

Join our club of magnetic women who are committed to creating intimate and passionate relationships; you'll find details on the back of this book.

Create your own community of women who are there to live and love to the fullest. It is very hard to see our own blind spots, and that's how we get stuck. With the help of your support team, you can jump obstacles and uncover blind spots much faster.

Interesting—now that I'm reading my book over again, it feels like I've written all of this for myself. It reminds me that knowing is not enough. I have to practice and live this wisdom every day. Wow, what an exciting journey!

Your Chance to Receive Tarisha's Expert Advice to Transform Your Relationship

Beautiful Woman, are you ready to deepen the intimacy with your partner and enjoy a magical loving relationship?

If you sense the possibility to rapidly transform your relationship with my personal support then I'd love to hear from you!

Apply for a complimentary "Get the Love You Desire" Breakthrough Session

- ❖ We'll work together to create a **crystal-clear vision for the kind of a relationship you'd like** to have with your partner;
- ❖ You'll **uncover hidden challenges** that may be sabotaging your success with creating the love life you dream about;
- ❖ You'll **leave the session renewed, reenergised** and **inspired** to finally create the relationship you desire

You will come out of this powerful session with:

- ☑ **Written positive outcomes** for your relationship;
- ☑ A **new awareness** of what is causing many **of the challenges** in your relationship right now (they may not be what you think!);
- ☑ A **renewed sense of energy** about turning your relationship around;
- ☑ A **"next-step" action plan** for moving your relationship into the next phase of love, intimacy and passion!

To apply for a complimentary "**Get the Love You Desire**" session, visit my website **www.deeplyinloveagain.com/breakthrough.**

You don't have to leave your house for the session, we will talk on the phone or Skype; so it doesn't matter where you are in the world!

Congratulations on your new intimate, passionate and deeply satisfying relationship!

Warmly,

Tarisha Tourok
Re-Ignite Your Love Coach
www.deeplyinloveagain.com/breakthrough

Bibliography

1. al-Khayyat, Sana. *Honour & Shame: Women In Modern Iraq*, 2001 Saqi Books.
2. Anand, Margo. *The Art of Sexual Ecstasy: The Path of Sacred Sexuality for Western Lovers*, 1992 Musselburgh: Scotprint Ltd.
3. Chalker, Rebecca. *The Clitoral Truth: The Secret World at Your Fingertips*, 2000 New York: Seven Stories Press.
4. Chia, Mantak & Abrams, Douglas. *The Multi-Orgasmic Man: Sexual Secrets Every Man Should Know*, 1997 New York: HarperCollins Publishers.
5. Chia, Mantak & Abrams, Rachel Carlton. *The Multi-Orgasmic Woman: Sexual Secrets Every Woman Should Know*, 2009 New York: HarperOne.
6. Farley, Sister Margaret A. *Just Love: A Framework for Christian Sexual Ethics*, 2008 London: Continuum.
7. Gray, John. *Men are from Mars, Women are from Venus*, 1995 New York: HarperCollins.
8. Hendrix, Harville Ph.D. *Getting the Love You Want—A Guide for Couples*, 1988 New York: Henry Holt.
9. Hite, Shere. *The Hite Report: A National Study of Female Sexuality*, 1976 New York: Macmillan Publishing Co.
10. Judith, Anodea. *Wheels of Life: A User's Guide to Chakra System*, 1999 Woodbury: Llewellyn Publications.

11. Krishnananda. *Face to Face with Fear: A Loving Journey From Co-Dependency to Freedom*, 1998 Kaisheim: Koregaon Publications.
12. Lloyd, J William *The Karezza Method*, www.reuniting.info/download/pdf/TheKarezzaMethodfv.pdf.
13. Madanes, Cloe. *Relationship Breakthrough—How to Create Outstanding Relationships in Every Area of Your Life*, 2009 New York: Rodale Inc.
14. Osho. *From Sex to Superconsciousness*, 2006 Pune: Tao Publishing.
15. Osho. *The Book of Secrets*, 1974 New York: St. Martin's Griffin.
16. Prescott, James W. *Body Pleasure and the Origins of Violence*, www.violence.de/prescott/bulletin/article.html.
17. Robinson, Marnia. *Cupid's Poisoned Arrow: From Habit to Harmony in Sexual Relationships*, 2009 Berkeley: North Atlantic Books.
18. Rosenthal, Joshua. *Integrative Nutrition*, 2007 New York: Integrative Nutrition Publishing.
19. Ryan Christopher and Jetha, Cacilda. *Sex at Dawn: The Prehistoric Origins of Modern Sexuality*, 2010 New York: HarperCollins Publishers.
20. Schnarch, David PH.D. *Passionate Marriage: Keeping Love and Intimacy Alive in Committed Relationships*, 2012 Brunswick: Scribe Publications.
21. Thomas, Katherine Woodward. *Calling in 'The One*, 2004 New York: Three Rivers Press.
22. Williamson, Marianne. *Enchanted Love: The Mystical Power of Intimate Relationships*, 1999 New York: Simon & Schuster Paperbacks.
23. Winston, Sheri: *Women's Anatomy of Arousal: Secret Maps to Buried Pleasure*, 2010 New York: Mango Garden Press.

What Tarisha's Clients Say

"I understand my husband so much better now"

"My relationship with my husband **was almost destroyed**. With Tarisha's help **I understand my husband so much better now, and I'm so much more connected to myself. The intimacy between us now is so much deeper, a whole new level**. Thank you! Thank you for your love and care, Tarisha."

Tatiana, Auckland, New Zealand

"I feel like I was given a new life."

"I can't believe my relationship with my husband changed so much! **We are again in love as twenty years ago,** but now this feels so much deeper. Wow! Where were you before, Tarisha? **I feel like I was given a new life."**

Susan, Auckland, New Zealand

"In all fourteen years of our marriage, I never felt so much love and intimacy"

"Before working with Tarisha, **I was stuck** in one place and felt unhappy. I was so tired and started to wait for the night to come in the morning. My relationship with my husband was good, but **we didn't have much excitement**, and I thought it was because of our children and not enough time.

How wrong I was! The workshop **changed my relationship so profoundly**! In all fourteen years, I never felt so much love and connection with my husband. Our love is so much deeper now. **The intimacy we created** using Tarisha's practices **is beyond all words**. Somehow, we even have more time for each other now. We are smiling more, and we are much more relaxed. Amazing how me going to the event changed my husband as well. He was stressed and overworked, but now he radiates joy and love. Wow! Just in one weekend! Where were you before, Tarisha? I feel like I was given a new life, I'm soooo happy.

Dear Woman, if you want to know more about your strength, your possibilities, and your beauty, this is a right place to start. You can explore your own senses, dreams, and hidden valleys with Tarisha's help. It's all here in you, and all you need is some guidance. And it's always good to spend time with like-minded women. I'm still discovering the depth of my love for my husband and myself."

Barbara D, Auckland, New Zealand

"Tarisha Really Understands What Men and Women Need"

"Almost immediately after Tarisha arrived at our weekly Essentially Men group for a talk about relationships between men and women, a new energy seemed to take hold of our group . . . We enjoyed rich, honest discussion about men's and women's needs, and it was fascinating to explore the male-female dynamic. I gained powerful insights into my relationship with my partner, and I feel as if I understand women better now. It was an uplifting and illuminating experience!"

Eric Atwood, Auckland, Essentially Men

"My relationship had changed markedly, and my wife says to me, "Now you get it!" We are intimate with each other. I feel wanted and significant."

Before I went to coaching from Tarisha, **my relationship of nearly thirty years was at an all time low** (and had been for while). We rarely were intimate with each other and **sex was almost nonexistent**.

I had read loads of books on the topic and done couple and individual counselling in the past with little effect. My wife would say to me about our love life and relationship, "You just don't get it do you?" And she was right! But she didn't seem to want to help out by telling me "what I didn't get."

From my perspective **I wasn't getting the love and connection I desired** from our relationship, and my being a nice, loving man, helping out at home, or doing things with our children had no or minimal effect on how things were.

In my work as a mechanic, when a customer brings their vehicle in, I often know what is wrong within a few minutes of checking the vehicle over. Tarisha was like that about my relationship with my wife. **After a few sessions with Tarisha, my relationship had changed markedly, and my wife can now be heard saying to me, "Now you get it!"** Or "Now you're talking my language!" **We are intimate with each other and make love. I feel wanted and significant.**

The key for me, with Tarisha's guidance, was **understanding what was going on inside me and learning about myself.** Then Tarisha's unique intuition and relationship knowledge guided me to **learn the language that had been there all along, that my wife had been "trying to tell me!"**

William, Auckland, New Zealand

My Gift to You

My special reader, here is my gift to you to complement this book—full scholarship to my virtual bootcamp valued at $97.

"Secrets That Men Would Never Tell You—What Do You Need to Know About Men to Have a Harmonious Relationship"

To receive access to my virtual bootcamp go to: www.deeplyinloveagain.com/bookgift

The Bootcamp Reveals . . .

- ☑ What to say to your man to **awaken his desire** for you
- ☑ How to get what you need from your man *without* sounding needy or demanding
- ☑ How to figure out why he is ignoring you and what you can do about it
- ☑ Why he looks at other women, what does it mean, and what can you do about it
- ☑ The #1 mistake that kills the passion in most relationships

I look forward to supporting you!

My warmest wishes to creating a fulfilling relationship with your man,

>Tarisha Tourok
>Re-Ignite Your Love Coach
>www.deeplyinloveagain.com/bookgift

About the Author

Tarisha's dream is to see every woman, YOU, overflowing with joy and being deeply, totally and completely in love with yourself just the way you are.

Isn't it time you CELEBRATE YOURSELF!

Tarisha's passion is to:

- Help you to step into **your sensuality and feminine power**
- Help you **appreciate your body and fall in love with yourself**
- Support you in **creating passionate** and **fulfilling relationship** with your man
- Help you to understand your man better
- **Deepen the intimacy** and create **excitement** in your love life
- Support you in **taking extra care of yourself**
- **Unleash a new level of confidence** in you

Tarisha's unique approach is highly experiential and allows you to unlock your sensuality and feminine power. This process gives you tools and wisdom to create loving, passionate, and flourishing relationships.

Tarisha has started her journey of self-discovery seven years ago by taking a very sharp turn when, one day, she heard a call to leave her normal life of security and sufficiency to go on a search of her own truth. At the time she was working in a Chartered Accountancy firm where she felt utterly miserable, constantly asking herself if that was what she was born for. She resigned and travelled to India to discover a different way of life, full of love and connection with others. Since then her life has changed dramatically: she discovered her inner power, felt blessed with being born as a woman, and, finally, realised she is beautiful.

Tarisha has a Bachelor of Commerce/Bachelor of Arts degree from the University of Auckland. She is a certified BioDynamic Breathwork practitioner, a sacred healer, and a holistic health coach certified by the American Association of Drugless Practitioners. She has participated in numerous self-growth workshops all around the world such as Awakening of Love, Tantra, Co-counselling, Pulsation, Satori self-inquiry, Childhood de-conditioning, Mystic Rose, Rebirthing, etc.

Tarisha lives in Auckland, New Zealand, with her beloved man and daughter. She runs workshops and gives private sessions to support people in creating intimacy and love in their relationships. In her spare time she likes skiing, sailing, hiking, talking to her chickens, and singing to the ocean.